# PASTORAL THEOLOGY
# FOR PUBLIC MINISTRY

# PASTORAL THEOLOGY FOR PUBLIC MINISTRY

*STEPHEN BURNS*

Seabury Books
NEW YORK

Unless otherwise noted, the Scripture quotations contained herein are from the New Revised Standard Version Bible, copyright © 1989 by the Division of Christian Education of the National Council of Churches of Christ in the U.S.A. Used by permission. All rights reserved.

Library of Congress Cataloging-in-Publication Data

Burns, Stephen, 1970-
  Pastoral theology for public ministry / Stephen Burns.
     pages cm
  Includes bibliographical references.
   ISBN 978-1-59627-264-4 (pbk.) — ISBN 978-1-59627-265-1 (ebook)  1. City churches. 2. City missions. 3. Cities and towns—Religious aspects—Christianity. 4. Pastoral theology. I. Title.
  BV637.B87 2015
  253—dc23
                          2015019414

Seabury Books
19 East 34th Street
New York, New York 10016

www.churchpublishing.org

An imprint of Church Publishing Incorporated

*Printed in the United States of America*

# CONTENTS

# INTRODUCTION

PASTORAL: used for the keeping or grazing of sheep or cattle:[1]

"What does your wife do?"

"She's a rector."

"Oh, my wife loves cooking, too. She loves anything to do with the kitchen."

The salesman in the car showroom evidently did not know what a "rector" was. And perhaps I should not have assumed that he would. Presumably Earl, the salesman, did not know Latin, and so did not know that we get "rector" from *regere*. Of course, even if he had, the clue was not there that this word—which means "ruler"—describes the profession of a certain kind of clergyperson. Indeed, as Gordon Lathrop reminds us, "rector" is hardly a good word to describe the work of a Christian minister.[2] It is one of what he calls "broken titles," along with "reverend," "father," "priest," "presbyter," and "minister," among others. Each broken title, Lathrop suggests, is problematic for its own reasons.

---

1. http://www.oxforddictionaries.com/definition/english/pastoral.
2. Gordon W. Lathrop, *The Pastor: A Spirituality* (Minneapolis, MN: Fortress Press, 2006), 9. Lathrop's book, and especially its introduction portion of "the pastor's lifelong catechumenate," is brilliant.

How could I have started to explain the work of a rector to Earl? He himself had told me that he was of Filipino heritage, and so perhaps he had some Christian background, but he obviously did not have enough to know the insider-speak of Episcopal church-talk. And would "pastor"—Lathrop's preferred word amongst the broken titles—have made anything clearer, given that it too comes from Latin, referring to one who looks after herds?

What, if anything, does this vignette suggest? Maybe only that we cannot assume that the role of the clergy is obvious to those outside a certain experience and worldview, perhaps an orbit that is getting smaller. Who, in fact, could doubt that?

I joined the train when it was quiet, with only a handful of people dispersed around the carriage. Station by station, passengers joined and the train filled up with people. The seats were arranged in different kinds of ways, with those where I sat in configurations for four persons. I wondered for a while why people sat everywhere else but with me in the four seats, even standing in the aisle. The journey itself was one I made often, and this was not behavior that I was used to seeing. And then I became conscious that I was wearing a clerical collar. Had people avoided me because of it? Was this symbol, intended to invite ministry, warding people off? What did they think I represented? What associations did the collar invite? At the time, wondering, I remembered a speech by the Archbishop of Canterbury to the UK Evangelical Alliance: people under thirty-five now not only found the church's rejection of homosexual persons incomprehensible, they found it wicked.[3] Was I identified with that oppression? And then I considered that Boston had been a storm center for stories of abuse by clerics, and had seen a subsequent hemorrhaging of the local Roman Catholic worshiping population. Was I being seen in that light? Was this very literal space around symbols

---

3. For versions of news coverage, see www.theguardian.com/uk-news/2013/28/gay-marriage -opposition-wicked-archbishop and www.telegraph.co.uk/news/religion/10271438/Arch bishop-urges-Christians-to-repent-over-wicked-attitude-to-homosexuality.html. Reporting of the address varied across the national press and a video of the speech can be found at the Evangelical Alliance website: www.eauk.org/church/stories/address-by-the -archbishop-of-canterbury.cfm (all websites accessed April 27, 2015).

of ministry a gesture of mistrust, disgust, at the very least caution? It is difficult to deny that the churches' failures to protect the vulnerable young have greatly damaged their reputation, and not least their audacity to pronounce on loving gay people's sexual practices. What is the day-to-day impact of this on those who bear Christian symbols in public space? This train ride was, for me, a rude awakening. It has continued to resonate with more recent experiences: for example, reading what a Hollywood actor has said about her "elation" that a church in my neighborhood was burned to the ground by an arsonist. She had attended the church as a child, witnessed the abuse of peers and friends, been caught up in the trauma caused to the community, moved away but managed to retain a discipline of worship elsewhere, and thinks that the destruction of the building is a "relief."[4]

The role of public ministers in public space is ever more ambiguous, as I think these brief vignettes suggest. The role of the churches in public debate—including "moral issues"—is as contentious as ever. Yet the response to these realities cannot be retreat by the churches into ecclesial enclaves of one kind or another, withdrawal from the wider public world. Anglican tradition at least has very little in its history to support any such move. So how should we think of the role of the public minister in public space? This is an important question in our changing context. And so *Pastoral Theology for Public Ministry* invites reflection on the role of ministers of the church, and it does so in two different but related ways.

## Narration of Steps

### Part One: Pastoral Theology

Part one offers an introduction to some of the main contours of the academic discipline of pastoral theology. How pastoral care and ministry are understood is related to what theological vision and resources

---

4. For versions of news coverage, see www.theage.com.au/victoria./fire-at-st-james
-church-in-brighton-a-relief-says-actor-rachel-griffiths-20150330-1mawmo.html
and www.abc.net.au/news/2015-03-3haunted-house-on-hill-rachel-griffiths-describes-
church-abuse/6357960.

are available to enable ministry. So the first three chapters are a way of telling the story of how pastoral theology is the way it is, what some of its main trajectories are, and where tensions exist within the discipline. Part one articulates key ways in which, in recent decades, pastoral theology has experienced a self-conscious transformation "from hints and tips to hermeneutics."[5] Hence it places different approaches to, different traditions of, pastoral theology side by side and sets them in conversation with one another. Naming these foci "traditions" emerges out of my attention to aspects of their history, their association with particular persons in particular settings, and their developments over time. We will call these traditions the "therapeutic," "classical," and "liberationist," and these are the focus of chapters 1–3, in turn. In narrating the concerns of these traditions, I introduce various theologians whose work exerts influence on the discipline: These thinkers range from figures such as Gregory the Great in the sixth century, George Herbert in the fifteenth century, and Anton Boisen in the twentieth century. We will employ perspectives from many important present-day pastoral theologians from across an ecumenical spectrum: Elaine Graham, Emmanuel Lartey, Gordon Lathrop, Bonnie Miller-McLemore, Thomas Oden, and Stephen Pattison among them. These writers are women and men, of different ethnicities, ordained and lay, from North America and elsewhere. As well as exploring the hermeneutics associated with therapeutic, classical, and liberationist traditions of pastoral theology, we will relate the traditions to particular images which I mean to be seen *together* in order to suggest the broad orbit of ministry. Most importantly, while the "altar" might stand at the center of church, references to hospital and road-work are meant to assert that pastoral care moves beyond congregational domains of ministry. So as the explorations of part one develop, they press toward a view of pastoral care and pastoral theology as public work, with eyes open to various demanding contexts in which public

---

5. Stephen Pattison and Gordon Lynch, "Pastoral and Practical Theology," in *The Modern Theologians: An Introduction to Christian Theology since 1918*, ed. David F. Ford with Rachel Muers (Oxford: Blackwell, 2005), 408.

ministry is practiced. None of this, of course, could be simply put to use to enter into a conversation with individuals such as Earl who did not know what a rector is, but it does, I hope, enable some confidence about what resources are available to ministers to frame and reframe their understanding of what they are doing.

## Part Two: Public Ministry

Part two of the book is especially concerned to underline the representative and symbolic dimensions of pastoral care. These are important to help orient the minister in public space. As the vignette of my train journey suggests, questions of what ministers represent are fraught with associations of prejudice and abuse in the church. So it is imperative to think through what symbols of ministry might best intend, what representation might involve at its best as well as at its worst. Notwithstanding that ministry moves beyond the congregational domain, the representative dimensions of ministry are concentrated and best learned at the center of congregational life—at the altar table, in the place of word and sacrament. The discussion, therefore, is not simply about documents and what might be made of them, however important those documents may be. It is *not* intended simply as an "academic" discussion of pastoral theology, but intentional about the ways in which liturgy and spirituality resource pastoral care. If, as suggested in part one, ministry has very wide *scope*, part two invites reflection on ways that Christian ministry finds its *focus*, but this is emphatically not to narrow "ministry" to "ordained ministry." On the contrary, the baptismal ecclesiology that has been fostered by contemporary ecumenical renewal rightly asserts that ministry belongs to all God's people. With that conviction, "pastoral care" may be part of baptismal ministry. But pastoral care, whoever exercises it, is always in some way related to word and table and, inevitably, this cluster of convictions does invite exploration of what might be so distinctive and demanding about ordained ministry. In part two, then, chapters 4 and 5 reflect on the caregiver as person and as symbol, and hence that pastoral ministry always involves dynamics of being not only "always oneself" but also "never only oneself." Just as part one draws on an ecumenical spectrum of theologians, so part two explores an ecumenical array of liturgical resources. That being said, chapter 4 offers a particular focus on the Episcopal Church's Book of Common Prayer 1979, exploring its Baptismal Covenant and some rubrics around the celebration of the Eucharist, making for a more intensive example that reflects my understanding of representative ministry being learned in liturgy.

### Criss-Crossing, Sloping

While, for some, this terrain may be new, my thinking is that some of the perspectives introduced in this book are riches from the past that are at risk of being forgotten but which are helpful for orienting ministers at the present time. This is particularly so with respect to the potential for ministry beyond the congregational domain and the symbolic freight of pastoral care. So I want to lay foundations for thinking about pastoral practice and for further exploration in practical theology, but to do so by looking at pastoral theology and public ministry emphatically *together*. Although there are particular emphases in each part and each chapter of what follows, there is also an intentional—perhaps inevitable—amount of criss-crossing and sloping from one focus to another.

To a certain extent, this can be seen as an alliance with a style of pastoral theology that I value and that resists too much systematization. One of the manifestations of this is that I have tried to press weight toward opening up discussion, rather than always stating my own conclusions. Another is in the stories I tell. This emphasis is also because I personally constantly navigate different cultures with their different mores, and I appreciate the breadth of the Anglican tradition, its ecumenical alliances, and different church styles. So I hope that I have found a "passionate balance"[6] between asking questions, making connections, telling stories, and stating personal convictions.

It is also the case that part one is more abstract than part two, and even as it is concerned with representative ministry, part two is at points

---

6. For this image, see Alan Bartlett, *A Passionate Balance: The Anglican Tradition* (Maryknoll, NY: Orbis, 2007).

quite personal, as seems to me to be apt to reflection on being "always oneself, never only oneself."

I confess that I have written *Pastoral Theology for Public Ministry* in the hope that it will be encouraging for students in seminaries, enabling reflection on the vocation they are entering and engendering appreciation of the rich resources at their disposal. I will, of course, be glad if ministers, lay and ordained, in different contexts, also find it helpful. Still, I am most grateful to students who at United Theological College in Sydney, New South Wales, Australia, and Episcopal Divinity School in Cambridge, Massachusetts, USA, have recently studied together with me in classes on pastoral theology, sacramental care, ordination studies, and various kinds of directed reading, dissertations, and other study projects that touch on the themes of this book. Many—but by no means all— of those present in classrooms were, of course, candidates for ordained ministries, with whom I have also shared in liturgy and, in some cases, deep spiritual conversation. I hope that this book conveys my great respect and affection for those students with whom I have been enormously privileged to learn and worship. I hope that this book emboldens them, and nurtures confidence about the possibility of intentional, self-conscious, representative ministry with a wide orbit.

# PART ONE

# PASTORAL THEOLOGY

## Resources for the Task

The next chapter will focus on hospitals, and specifically the wards of psychiatric hospitals where the origins of the therapeutic tradition of pastoral theology are to be found, but I would like to begin with a few words of perspective on the task of part one as a whole. Part one surveys three different, but related, traditions of pastoral theology. I call these traditions the therapeutic, the classical, and the liberationist, and the place to begin to think about them side by side is not quite the psychiatric ward, but the optometrist's clinic.

Having one's eyes tested by an optometrist is an experience of clarifying vision. During an eye test, one is asked to read a sequence of letters of ever-decreasing size, with the help of different lenses as needed. Spectacle frames may be perched upon the patient's face, and lens after lens used to see how it enables sight. Sometimes specialized optometrist frames may hold several lenses at a time, so that one lens is placed in front of another, and another in front of that, all the time to bring vision into focus. As different lenses are tried out, with patience and skill, vision sharpens.

It may be helpful to hold on to this image of the optometrist's clinic through what follows in part one. The three traditions about to be surveyed suggest different "lenses" to bring to perusal of pastoral care, different ways of seeing it. One particular lens or another may help to shape vision of a particular pastoral care setting and scenario. We will look through these three lenses, in order to suggest that there is *always more than one way of looking* at and considering a pastoral situation. Moreover, it is not just that the lenses may be viewed one at a time, but that for sharp vision of things, *multiple lenses* may need to be used in conjunction with one another. So the therapeutic tradition which is central to chapter 1 may need to be overlaid with what chapter 2 calls the classical tradition, which may further need to be seen from what chapter 3 calls a liberationist perspective. Looking through one lens may bring clarity to a pastoral situation, and enable pastoral action, but it might also be necessary to look through all three lenses, or the lenses in different combinations, to see a situation as clearly as possible. The optometrist's multifocal spectacles need to be remembered as one stands in any particular place and their multifocal vision needs to be carried between such settings in one's imagination.

On to the hospital.

# CHAPTER 1

# Reading the Living Human Document: A Therapeutic Tradition

With this chapter, we open up the first of three styles or traditions of pastoral care: the therapeutic, which comes first in as a broadly chronological sketch, with classical and liberationist traditions following. This chronology reflects the way in which each tradition emerged through the twentieth century. In what follows, then, the three traditions are presented in a construct that suggests their historical emergence as distinctive emphases through the last century, each of which remain viable in the twenty-first century, and all of which draw on long, even ancient, precedents in the practice of pastoral care and the durable sources of theology in scripture and tradition.

The therapeutic tradition is illumined by the image of "reading the living human document." The phrase "living human document" is central to this tradition, and is one of its gifts and challenges to the practice of pastoral care. In order to understand its significance, we need to focus on the ministry of one particular Presbyterian minister in New England in the United States of America in the first decades of the twentieth century, Anton T. Boisen. Boisen lived to be nearly ninety years old, and by the time of his death in 1965 he had left a huge legacy to the church in the form of a program of pastoral training for ministers that came to be known as Clinical Pastoral Education.

## Opportune Madness

Anton Boisen was born in 1876 in Bloomington, Indiana, the child of parents who had emigrated from Germany in the decade before his birth. Both of his parents were involved in the University of Indiana: His father taught modern languages (an area in which Anton would study) and his mother was among the first cohort of women to attend the university as students. Members of Boisen's extended family were also involved in the work of the university: His grandfather was professor of math and a cousin of his grandfather was the university's first president. Boisen's father died when Anton was seven years old, and one particular other person also involved in the university, a Dr. William Bryan, came to be something of a surrogate father to him. This relationship was very important in Boisen's youth, and remained so throughout his life. His autobiography, *Out of the Depths*, is dedicated to Bryan, as "teacher and friend." Bryan was professor of philosophy and psychology and he encouraged Boisen to study psychology as an undergraduate, as well as supervising some of Boisen's postgraduate work in that field. While unsurprisingly his father's death during his childhood years left a profound and enduring mark on the son, the wider academic context of his upbringing is also important, as it underlines Boisen's familiarity with a milieu in which he later sought and found influence himself.

As a young man, Boisen—a person with "a preoccupied mind and a distant personality"[1]—was engaged in numerous lines of work, including things as diverse as modern languages (like his father), ordained ministry (like a number of others in his extended family), forestry, and ethnography, according to biographers. However, in all of these activities he "had

---

1. Henri Nouwen, "Anton Boisen and Theology Through Living Human Documents," in *Vision from a Little Known Country: A Boisen Reader*, ed. Glenn H. Asquith, Jr. (Decatur, GA: Journal of Pastoral Care Publications, 1992), 158.

not found his vocation."[2] At age forty-four, Boisen experienced some kind of major mental disorientation that led to his hospitalization in a psychiatric institution. This important personal experience in Boisen's life stands behind the pastoral theologian Robert Dykstra's depiction of pastoral theology being "born in madness."[3]

As he was to narrate in a substantial theological memoir of his experience published in 1936, *The Exploration of the Inner World*, Boisen came to understand the problem which led to his illness in terms of a sense of unfulfilled vocation—what he called his "years of wandering." He also made clear that a more immediate presenting problem was a sometimes intense preoccupation with masturbation. Again in *Exploration of the Inner World*, he wrote, "The realm of sex was for me at once fascinating and terrifying,"[4] and he was overwhelmed by it. In part, he was overwhelmed because his "sexual interests could neither be controlled nor acknowledged for fear of condemnation"[5] in the religious environment in which he was raised. But at least on reflection, it seems that he understood this interest in "sex-organ excitement"—that apparently preoccupied him from the age of four—as a manifestation of the deeper distraction: his vocational "wandering." It is clear from his reflections, too, that in his adulthood both his vocational and sexual frustration clustered around one particular woman. *Out of the Depths* indicates that he harbored a lifelong love of Alice Batchelder, which remained unrequited, and utterly consuming. Boisen himself suggested that his religious faith was "interwoven" with his love for Alice, just as it was with his memory of his father. For her part, Alice "sensed that Boisen needed her, if not as a wife, then certainly as a point around which to center his life."[6] In any case, when Boisen's various wanderings led to an inability to function in his professional work and in the domestic sphere, his family arranged for him to be admitted against his will at Boston

---

2. Nouwen, "Boisen," 159.
3. Robert C. Dykstra, *Images of Pastoral Care: Classic Readings* (St. Louis, MO: Chalice Press), 2.
4. Dykstra, *Images*, 228, note 1.
5. Dykstra, *Images*, 228, note 1.
6. Nouwen, "Boisen," 167.

Psychopathic Hospital in Massachusetts. He was diagnosed with violent delirium and was considered to be a severe case from which recovery would be quite unlikely. A week later, he was transferred to Westboro State Hospital. Yet despite the initial diagnosis of severe delirium, and much to the surprise of his psychiatrists and the clinical team responsible for his care, Boisen was soon well enough to be discharged. As it happened Boisen was able to be given a choice to leave the institution within a matter of weeks. He chose to stay and remained a patient there for fifteen months.

Remarkably, Boisen chose, *over time*, to stay for extended periods over the next years, to live in the kind of therapeutic community in which he had initially been confined against his will. That is, although he was never forcibly admitted again, and so was always free to leave, Boisen chose to spend much of his life in institutions like the one in which he had been a patient. Sometimes he lived in such institutions in roles as chaplain, and at other times chose to live in hospitals as a patient. In 1924, four years after his breakdown, he was appointed as chaplain to a psychiatric institution, Worcester State Hospital, and chose to live in the hospital in his chaplaincy role. Later, when Boisen began to pioneer training programs for clergy working in hospitals, he again chose to remain living in hospitals.[7] In other words, as Henri Nouwen—one of Boisen's students and biographers—noted, Boisen "made his own illness the focus of his life."[8]

However strange it may have seemed to others, for his own part, Boisen regarded his hospital experience positively. As he said, "To be plunged as a patient into a hospital for the insane may be a tragedy or an opportunity. For me it was an opportunity."[9] He saw it as the opportunity to understand the experience of mental illness.

As Boisen was later able to reflect on his initial hospitalization in relation to what he saw of others living closely with him in hospital

---

7. Nouwen, "Boisen," 159.
8. Nouwen, "Boisen," 159.
9. Anton T. Boisen, *Exploration of the Inner World* (Philadelphia: University of Pennsylvania Press, 1971), 1.

situations, he came to think that mental illness was a matter of the patient's inner world becoming disorganized. He stated what he came to see as a common problem for many persons in these terms:

> Something ha[d] happened which ha[d] upset the foundations upon which his (sic) ordinary reasoning is based. Death or disappointment or sense of failure may have compelled a reconstruction of the patient's worldview from the bottom up, and the mind becomes dominated by the one idea, which he has been trying to put in its proper place.[10]

For Boisen himself, his disappointment centered on his unrequited love for Alice; this had become the "dominating idea" which felled him.

## Boisen's Courage

Boisen was presumably at least partially aware of his own needs in choosing to make psychiatric hospitals his home, but his decision nevertheless took courage. This courage marked his later life as profoundly as his sexual preoccupations had marked his adolescence and young adulthood, and in one notable piece of testimony he likened his adventurous approach to a willingness to get lost: "It is only the dubs who never go five miles from camp, who don't get lost sometimes."[11] And

> for me to stick right to camp and wash dishes all the rest of my life for fear of getting lost again would take out of life all that makes it worth living for me. I am not afraid. I have always managed to find my way through; and I do think that in a very real sense I have been exploring some little known territory, which I should like now to have a chance to map out.[12]

Over time, Boisen became convinced that problems commonly diagnosed as medical were in fact, or at least in part, religious[13]—as in his

---

10. Dykstra, *Images*, 29.
11. A quotation from a friend, cited with approval by Boisen; Dykstra, *Images*, 27.
12. Dykstra, *Images*, 27.
13. Dykstra, *Images*, 26.

own troubles with sex—and he was concerned about what he perceived as the failure of psychiatrists to engage with the religious dimensions of the mentally distressed and the failure of Christian pastors to engage with the terrain in which psychiatrists worked. Boisen's concerns about pastors were both that they had little or no opportunity to engage institutionally in ministry in psychiatric hospitals and that they had little or no training or skill to engage personally in journeying with others into their "inner world" of religiously related trauma. Religious language and religious practice were media through which disorder might be manifest. Hence, on the one hand, Boisen wrote, "I feel that many forms of insanity are religious rather than medical problems and that they cannot be successfully treated until they are so recognized."[14] He saw the key problem of many persons in psychiatric hospitals as that of not having resolved "inner conflicts like that which Paul describes in the famous passage in the seventh chapter of Romans"[15]—"I do not do what I want, but I do the very thing I hate" (Romans 7:15). So while the church may have believed and proclaimed that this Pauline conflict could be overcome, it is clear that some people struggle hard to resolve it, breaking down in the attempt. Psychiatric patients are those who have come to "unhappy solutions which thus far the church has ignored."[16] On the other hand, Boisen felt that the kindly but inept ministers who conducted services in the hospital "might know something about religion, but they certainly knew nothing about our problems."[17] As an example of what he meant, he related a story about one such minister preaching on the gospel text "If your right eye causes you to sin, tear it out" (Matthew 5:29) to a congregation of persons in mental distress. But Boisen also recognized that the fact that ministers might simply take services but not visit on the wards was not simply their fault: "They probably received little encouragement to do so."[18] Indeed, it was his own experience that when he looked for a ministry position in hospital chaplaincy, there were no available options. He decided therefore to take a job

---

14. Dykstra, *Images*, 26.
15. Dykstra, *Images*, 25.
16. Dykstra, *Images*, 25.
17. Dykstra, *Images*, 25.
18. Dykstra, *Images*, 25.

in the psychological department (and later the social services department) of a hospital. It was only after some time that he was able to move from that position into a chaplaincy role. Boisen's life was marked not only by the courage to "get lost," but also by the patience and persistence to find ways toward the opportunities he sought.

## Boisen's Vision

The events of Boisen's life turned him from various lines of unproductive work toward enormously fruitful service in the context of a sector ministry in psychiatric hospitals. During his time as a chaplain and resident in psychiatric hospitals and later as a seminary professor (then also residing in hospitals), Boisen developed what he called clinical pastoral training, which would come to have enormous influence on ministerial training in many traditions across continents for decades. What has for many years now been widely known as Clinical Pastoral Education is deeply dependent on Boisen's vision. Growing through collaboration with others from his own initial experience, programs of clinical pastoral training were Boisen's attempt to put right at least the lack of opportunity and encouragement for ministers to become engaged with persons living with mental illness. He began to host such programs as a chaplain, working in hospitals with seminarians who, as part of their training for Christian ministry, would encounter patients in psychiatric wards: They would do more than take services, but would also work on wards as ordinary attendants, spending time with patients, and being able to get to know persons by sharing something of their experience.

This model of close involvement with persons experiencing mental distress has become a mainstay of ministerial formation in mainline traditions in the United States. Clinical Pastoral Education (CPE) might now feature in the training of ministers beyond liberal Protestant traditions—including Roman Catholic or Pentecostal, for instance—to different extents. CPE can now also feature as a part of ministerial formation in other parts of the world rather than just in North America. While Boisen's model was focused on hospitals, asserting the role of the chaplain in an interdisciplinary clinical team (because "the chaplain is also a scientist, specialized in the religious aspects of the case under consideration"[19]) many other kinds of sector ministry, not only in hospitals, now embrace more or less of Boisen's legacy. So prison ministry, industrial chaplaincy, and forms of ministry in other contexts have learned from his vision of a need for ministers *to be present* in different arenas. Also forged from Boisen's vision of the chaplain's role in a psychiatric care team have been many other practices of chaplaincy in multidisciplinary teams in many different contexts.

## Reading the Living Human Document

Central to clinical pastoral training was Boisen's emphasis on attention to the experience of persons, themselves regarded by him as "living human documents." The now commonplace stress on the priority of experience in contemporary theology can be related to Boisen's initiatives. He developed the kinds of insight and convictions that have not only shaped his own and others' engagement with psychiatric institutions and other sector ministries, but that also engaged his academic theological colleagues as well as ministerial practitioners, and that have shaped a discipline within the theological curriculum for generations to follow: "practical theology."

Boisen used the phrase "the living human document" to turn attention from the study of texts in theology—scripture, historical documents, books of systematic theology, and so on—to human persons. As he said, "Theological students should have the opportunity to go to firsthand sources for their knowledge of human nature. I wanted them to learn to read living human documents as well as books."[20] So in Boisen's vision, patients—persons—were texts to be read. Notably, for Boisen, such reading of persons was not simply a case of the minister making observation about a person living with mental illness, but involved the minister having access to the patient's medical files, therapeutic team meetings about the patients' care (these days often called "case conferences"),

---

19. Nouwen, "Boisen," 170.
20. Dykstra, *Images*, 29.

and being engaged in dialogue with medical professionals. It involved inter-disciplinary, which is to say nontheological, sources and included these in theological reflection. Not only did Boisen want to turn theology toward persons as living documents, he also wanted theology to look to the insights of other fields of knowledge.

He was, therefore, a pioneer of an approach to theology that sought to decenter written texts, abstract ideas, or academic theories as the starting place of theological reflection and to replace them with the concrete realities of particular human lives. His example has not been uncontroversial, not only because of its obvious challenge to what many have long considered authorities for theological construction and correctness, but also because of his own seemingly minimal appreciation of theology. For while he was insistent that what were often understood as medical or psychiatric problems included religious dimensions that needed to be recognized, his own theological style was firmly embedded in the kind of liberal Protestantism in which he was raised. Indeed, his own interest did not extend very far in an explicitly doctrinal direction. As he said in his autobiography, "My own problems were not theological, they had to do with inner adjustments."[21] And when, later in life, he came to a point where he felt able to own a personal creed, it was a minimal one: "I believe that the paramount human need is that for love and that there is a law within which forbids us to be satisfied with any fellowship save that of the best."[22] In liberal theological environments, such as the one in which he had grown up and later taught ordinands, this perhaps rather modest role for theology and this bare creed may have been welcomed, but it has not always been the case in other environments.

## Revering the Living Human Document

Given that Boisen once taught theology in Chicago, it is apt that his approach fits well in the milieu of what would later come to be called the "Chicago School" of theology, identified with better-known

---

21. Anton T. Boisen, *Out of the Depths* (New York: Harper and Brothers, 1960), 39.
22. Boisen, *Depths*, 197.

theologians like David Tracey, a major force in liberal Catholicism in the latter decades of the twentieth century. For all their differences, mentioning Boisen together with Tracey invites reflection on ways in which pastoral theology is related to wider styles of theological thinking, which may or may not be considered by others to be pastoral theology. Boisen's theology shares marks associated with the so-called Chicago School, particularly its sense of theology's relation to wider cultures that is manifest in core aspects of its methods. This sense is most commonly traced to Paul Tillich's depiction of Christ and culture in correlation, such that culture was understood by Tillich to pose certain questions for which Christ has answers. Although Boisen himself did not develop a correlational theory like Tillich's or Tracey's, it is clear that he did not understand theology to be a singly authoritative source of insight and it is certainly the case that Boisen's methods continue to meet quite considerable resistance. As we shall see, the classical tradition of pastoral care is an example of a certain resistance to perceived weaknesses in a liberal, interdisciplinary, person-centered (as opposed to what is considered to be a God-centered) approach to theology. At the very least, however, this means that Boisen's notion of persons as living human documents is an immensely important feature shaping the discipline of pastoral theology, not only because some strands of the discipline have followed it, but because others have departed from it. Boisen's approach calls for close attention to persons, to the quest for shared wisdom and mutual accountabilities, which unnerves some. Others lean in to his approach, regarding it not just as a way of thinking, but as an approach that might even invite the descriptor "spirituality." As Charles Gerkin points out in his reflections on Boisen, the reading of persons as texts is a kind of spiritual practice: Persons as texts are not simply to be read, but to be *revered*, akin to holy books of deep tradition. So Gerkin elaborates:

> Anton Boisen's image of the human person as a "document" to be read and interpreted in a manner analogous to the interpretation of a historical text has . . . simply been taken as an admonition to begin with the experience of persons in the development of ministry theory. That certainly was central to Boisen's intention. Boisen, however, meant more than that. He meant that the

depth experience of persons in the struggles of their mental and spiritual life demanded the same respect as do the historic texts from which the foundations of our Judeo-Christian tradition are drawn. Each individual living human document has an integrity of his or her own that calls for understanding and interpretation, not categorisation and stereotyping. Just as the preacher should not look to proof texts to be twisted into the meaning sought for, so also the individual human text demanded a hearing on its own merit.[23]

Faced with such "texts," the pastoral caregiver's role is to respect, engage with, and pay close attention to the particular language, images, gestures, tone, timbre, and silences of the patient, in order to interpret the patient with care. So Gerkin's own contribution to the discipline of pastoral theology has been to develop Boisen's insight into a vision of pastoral care as "hermeneutics," and of the pastoral caregiver as "hermeneut." Notably, one of Gerkin's major books directly echoes Boisen's language before directing it in a more highly theorized way: *The Living Human Document: Re-Visioning Pastoral Counseling in a Hermeneutical Mode*.[24] In certain theological milieu, then, Boisen's phrase has sometimes come to take on considerable weight. Living human documents— persons and their words, their stories, their narratives—provide sources, even norms and indeed authorities, for theological enquiry. Human persons, even in some of the most troubling episodes of their lives, are, as it were, "the stuff of" theology. In the Boisen-ian mold, theology involves, alongside whatever written texts and abstract ideas and whatever strands of the history of ideas might be considered, the case study and concrete diagnosis of a living human document as a source of authority, and as worthy of reverence, in theological themes.

Interpretations of Boisen's terms, such as Gerkin's, have no doubt helped to shift the emphasis on living human documents out of clinical environments into the wider arenas of Christian ministry. Highlighting

---

23. Dykstra, *Images*, 34.
24. Charles V. Gerkin, *The Living Human Document: Re-Visioning Pastoral Counseling in Hermeneutical Mode* (Nashville, TN: Abingdon, 1984).

the resonance between scriptural and human persons as "texts" has supported Boisen's concern to be appropriated into congregational and other forms of ministry, as well as helping people to receive the ministry of pastoral interpretation of their experience in this particular way.

## Theological Method: Starting with Experience

As Gerkin notes, as Boisen's legacy has been shaped and reshaped in others' appropriation, it has commonly been read as insisting that pastoral care and pastoral theology *begin with* human experience. This dynamic is clearly depicted even in the title of the American United Methodist pastoral theologian John Patton's book *From Ministry to Theology: Pastoral Action and Reflection.*[25] Patton means to be very clear that ministry is prior to theology, and indeed gives rise to theology. In this view, theology is not the "application" of what might be learned in books to situations of ministry, but a process in which experience itself plays a crucial and constructive role. The subtitle of Patton's book reiterates a related dynamic: Action is prior to reflection, action leads to reflection. This is not to say that Patton, or Boisen, or others who could be identified within the therapeutic tradition are naïve or unsubtle in their thinking about ways in which action and reflection are in reality always interacting, perhaps messily. It is by no means that thought is excluded from action. Rather their key point, central to the whole therapeutic tradition that has evolved from Boisen's work, is that ministerial action is theoretically prior and primary to the theological "deposit" of scripture and other aspects of Christian tradition. As they understand process in pastoral theology in therapeutic style, pastoral caregivers and pastoral theologians turn to the Christian tradition after having paid their best attention to human experience as persons are articulating it for themselves and as it is perceived not only by their own but also by others' (such as psychiatrists') observation. As Patton elaborates on his own method, theology

---

25. John Patton, *From Ministry to Theology: Pastoral Action and Reflection* (Nashville, TN: Abingdon, 1991).

is "bracketed out" of at least the *initial* stages of pastoral action. This is to say that within the therapeutic tradition, pastoral care does not involve any quick or easy move to the invocation of specific Christian doctrines. They may be relevant, but they are consciously withheld until later stages of reflection on persons' need for care.

Patton's book is one example of how the conviction that doctrine may need to be bracketed out of the initial stages of pastoral care has shaped the methodology of much academic pastoral theology. It is now commonplace for pastoral theology to introduce doctrinal reflection only after first attempting to describe experience, to read a living human document. And while doctrinal reflection is not unimportant or unauthoritative for pastoral care shaped by the therapeutic tradition, it is the case that doctrinal reflection is unlikely to be regarded a final. Rather, in much pastoral theology, living human documents and the documents of the Christian tradition are kept in constant relationship. They may cohere with, or they may contest, each other, and the kind of methodology that is commonly used to allow either of these outcomes to be possible is often called "mutually critical correlation," a phrase of David Tracey's now much used in pastoral theology. In this method, different kinds of "document," different kinds of "story"—personal narrative, interdisciplinary perspectives, scriptural narrative, doctrinal perspectives—are all kept in play. It is not assumed that doctrinal or scriptural insights answer, silence, or settle issues raised in living human documents, though they may have a very significant role in interpreting situations. Rather, reflection on experience may also unsettle and reshape theological reflection, and doctrinal and scriptural understandings may be transformed, enlarged, or relinquished, through their interaction with living human documents.

## Adjusting Theology

One of the most striking outlines of mutually critical correlation is developed in an unflinching piece of reflection by the late Anthony Dyson, erstwhile professor of pastoral and social theology at Manchester

University in England. He relates the doctrine of the resurrection to the disease AIDS in a robust example of the way in which pastoral theology offers an "adjusting theology" that changes the apparent "correctness" of systematic theological thinking. Indeed, Dyson suggests "pastoral theology has now to be placed centrally in the pattern of the theological disciplines, thus ousting dogmatic theology and biblical theology."[26] Dyson's approach is to bring ideas about resurrection as a Christian doctrine—acknowledged in its diversity and ambiguity—and insight into AIDS both from the social sciences and from persons speaking from their own experience about living with the condition. Both of these features can be seen to be in clear continuity with the therapeutic tradition, which emphasizes interdisciplinarity and the importance of the living human document.

Dyson strongly commends the use of David Tracey's concept of mutually critical correlation in pastoral theology. Tracey nuanced Tillich's correlational methodology, regarding its unilateralism as overly simplistic. So, it is not that culture proposes a question that Christ somehow answers. Rather, Christ and culture are posed in reciprocal tension; there is a mutually critical correlation about the relationship between Christ and culture, or theology and culture, such that the supposed content of Christian doctrine—the meaning of Christ, say—can be exposed to question, critique, and change in the correlational process. Tracey emphasized such "mutually critical" dynamics as correctives to Tillich's earlier proposals about correlational method. He insisted that the correlation is not simply from a human situation to a theological response, but rather that the correlation may be mutually confronting: Theological ideas may be challenged by human situations. Pastoral theology, at least in the therapeutic tradition, is as interested in this latter dynamic as in the former, which can be one of the ways it is marked out from some other theological styles. So Tracey, quoted by Dyson, writes:

---

26. Anthony C. Dyson, "The Body of Christ Has AIDS," in *Resurrection: Essays in Honour of Leslie Houlden*, ed. Stephen Barton and Graham Stanton (London: SPCK, 1994), 173. The following paragraphs quote from pages 170–74 of Dyson's chapter.

[Pastoral] theology is . . . appropriately a generalist discipline that draws freely upon the specialized knowledge of many different, more narrowly structured perspectives and ways of accumulating knowledge about the world. That appropriation of specialized knowledge must, however, be a disciplined appropriation that is itself shaped by the process of mutually critical correlation which tests the perspectives of other narratives by their abrasion against the Christian narrative, even as that narrative is itself tested and reinterpreted.

It is important to point out that Tracey has in his turn been critiqued, such that the notion of "the Christian narrative" is less capable of gaining assent than at the time of his own using of this term. Latterly, questions about whose version of "the Christian narrative" is being proposed are also likely to be prominent, with possible determination to acknowledge versions of that narrative that had previously been excluded or withheld from wide awareness. Or put another way, in postmodern perspective, the idea that there is in fact a single narrative that can be referred to by the definite article ("*the* Christian narrative") is to invite suspicion that certain ways of narrating and certain narratives have eclipsed others, perhaps violently.

One of the most powerful features of Dyson's enactment of mutually critical correlation is the sense of the unrelenting challenge presented to doctrinal affirmations by the voices of persons articulating their experience for themselves. In Dyson's example of persons living with AIDS, he gathers counterperspectives to simple doctrinal affirmation: An example of their general tenor might be, "there is nothing good about it. There is nothing positive about it. It is painful, degrading, and fearful." In fact, Dyson juxtaposes fragment after fragment of such personal perspectives, so that the sense is of a forceful torrent of countertestimony to any simple ideas about hope on the basis of a doctrine of resurrection. Dyson introduces the outpouring he presents simply by saying that his presentation is "impressionistic." It is of course an impressionistic *construct*, but the impression given is immensely powerful, defying the sense that it is simply *ad hoc*. Indeed, it draws on a range of literary sources that cohere in the strength of their feeling.

When Dyson comes to relate such experience to the doctrine of resurrection, he suggests "we are to live out the dialectic of the Christian narrative and the narrative of HIV/AIDS in mutual abrasion and reinterpretation." In this, pastoral theology is affirmed as "the constitutive theological discipline, governed mainly by present-centered norms." Perhaps most challengingly, Dyson suggests that "we must find ways of dispensing with th[e theological] sediment in ways which open up contemporary, and often bitter, experience which proffers none or very little of that 'consolation' of resurrection that we have been led to believe is our portion and privilege." Here we see not just the doctrine of resurrection addressing experience, but a particular experience—that of AIDS—addressing, confrontationally, the doctrine.

Another challenging example of mutually critical correlation may be seen in a moving piece by Stephen Pattison on what he calls "the shadow side of Jesus." In this article, Pattison is critical of research on "the historical Jesus" which has sought to "exonerate . . . Jesus from his responsibility for the possibly less than good things which have been done in his name by the church."[27] Pattison insists that whatever doctrinal affirmations might be made about Jesus, "his life and teaching had a down, or shadow, side during the time of his own ministry."[28] Furthermore, he prioritizes that "Jesus is 'incarnated' in the church" over "whether or not God was incarnated in Jesus."[29] Some of the church's tendencies and sins are because Jesus was who he was with his particular shadow side. Pattison's pastoral theology therefore suggests some revisionist ideas about Jesus, at least of ideas about Jesus which fail to look at the ways in which the "legacy" of Jesus may be manifest in exclusivist and dehumanizing practices.

These different examples of "experience-based" approaches can be seen as illustrative of Emmanuel Lartey's assertion that pastoral theology

---

27. Stephen Pattison, *The Challenge of Practical Theology: Selected Essays* (London: Jessica Kingsley, 2007), 229.
28. Pattison, *Challenge*, 229.
29. Pattison, *Challenge*, 229.

resolutely refuses to ignore unpleasant human experience,[30] a charge
that pastoral theologians sometimes lay at the door of both biblical and
systematic theologies. Indeed, Boisen can be seen as inspiring a mode
of theology that learns from his courage as much as from his particular
method.

Perhaps at its most poignant, Boisen's approach can also be related
or extended to the kinds of theological responses that have emerged to
large-scale human tragedies like the Holocaust, for which even finding
language is so difficult.[31] Some theological responses to the inhuman
suffering of the Holocaust have stressed that the stories of survivors constitute something like "the stories of a new bible" which jar and grate
against scriptural/canonical/authorized/authoritative stories, which have
in a variety of liturgical settings so often been proclaimed as promis-
ing some sort of personal, national, global, or cosmic "happy ending,"
and in the context of systematic theology so often ordered in fore-
casts of eschatological fulfilment by divine design. The Holocaust narratives—which include convictions of, say, the abandonment of God,
the vacuity of divine "promise," of divine impotence to help persons in
their suffering, and of indictment of the Christian tradition for facilitat-
ing climates of anti-Semitism that enabled the Holocaust to happen—
challenge the authority of what Christian theologians oftentimes claim
to be their authorities in theologies, and scripture's role in tradition. In
the awful narratives of abuse in the Holocaust we have an acute example of what taking seriously Anton Boisen's challenge to attend to living
human documents *might* mean. Boisen lived through both World Wars
of the twentieth century and died in a period in which at least some of
those who had survived the Holocaust were able to have their memories and reflections published—Primo Levi and Elie Weisel being among

---

30. Emmanuel Y. Lartey, *Pastoral Theology in an Incultural World* (Cleveland, OH: Pilgrim Press, 2006), 101.

31. See Stephen Burns, "Forgiveness in Challenging Circumstances," in *Forgiveness in Context: Theology and Psychology in Creative Dialogue*, ed. Fraser Watts and Elisabeth Gulliford (London: Continuum, 2004), 144–59.

the best known examples.[32] Boisen did not himself apply his image of human persons as living human documents to the global events through which he lived. But the theological emphases and methods he promoted through Clinical Pastoral Education can indeed be related to wider issues. As Boisen's own vision has been appropriated, there has been a widening of the horizons he originally envisaged. His emphasis on individuals as living human documents continues to be worthy of much attention. Contextualized in his own life, this emphasis on individuals can be seen from different angles. On the one hand, it is the case that Boisen, who developed his theological reflection on his experience at the height of the so-called "social gospel" in the United States, meant his own emphasis to return attention to individuals. On the other hand, Boisen was consistently concerned to understand individuals in the setting of their wider relationships. Indeed, he remarked that a common characteristic of persons experiencing mental illness was their isolation from others "through a social judgment which either consciously or subconsciously they accept and pronounce upon themselves."[33] For his own part, he was acutely conscious of his personal successes and failures being dependent on gaining a sense of affinity with others. Living human documents, then, may be isolated, but at least part of the point and part of the task of reading them is to retrieve a sense of their wider bonds. The basis for a turn to attend to "the living human web," championed by feminist pastoral theologian Bonnie Miller-McLemore,[34] can be found in his own work.

## Turning to Other Traditions

Even when Boisen's own contribution is not foregrounded in the teaching of pastoral theology, it is likely to stand somewhere in the background as a very significant factor in why (pastoral) theology is being

32. See Isabel Wollaston, "'"Where He Is?" This Is Where—Hanging Here from This Gallows.' An Exploration of the Child-Hanging Scene in Elie Wiesel's *Night*,'" in *Exchanges of Grace: Essays in Honour of Ann Loades*, ed. Natalie K. Watson and Stephen Burns (London: SCM Press, 2008), 55–65.
33. Boisen, *Exploration*, 28.
34. Discussed below in relation to the liberationist tradition.

taught as it is, having been received into later approaches and resourcing their convictions. In his own ways, Boisen was a pioneer of interdisciplinarity in theological enterprise, seeking insight from beyond the orbit of established authorities of theological understanding. He—like the liberal tradition to which he belonged, and the forms of interdisciplinarity in theology for which he is in part responsible—have been much maligned in some quarters for this approach. The question of the centrality of experience remains a focus of discussion in pastoral theology, as well as a major point of controversy and contest with other disciplines within the theological curriculum. Sometimes experience is accepted as the central resource for theological construction, as in the bold articulation of Chung Hyun Kyong, writing about Asian women's experience. She suggests that such women—herself included—should "realize that we are the text, and the Bible and tradition of the Christian church are the context of our theology."[35] But at the same time criticism of such perspectives emerges in various ways—as diluting Christian theology, as looking in the wrong places for divine truth, as trusting ill-advisedly to so-called "secular" knowledge, as decentering supposedly "revealed" sources of theology—all perhaps different ways of stating a fundamental unease about whether interdisciplinarity can be properly, really, or fully Christian. Criticism has been particularly trenchant of ways in which Boisenesque alliance with human sciences (as opposed to the "divine science/art" of revealed theology?) might have led to the "therapeutic captivity" of theology. These criticisms lead the way to alternative proposals about pastoral theology, for the discipline of pastoral theology as a trajectory of academic enquiry has developed in critical appreciation of Boisen's legacy, not always accepting it in every aspect, as the very fact of other styles or "traditions"—what we will come to consider as "classical" and "liberationist," not least—testifies.

---

35. Quoted by Emmanuel Y. Lartey, *In Living Colour: An Intercultural Approach to Pastoral Care and Counseling* (London: Mowbray, 1997), 100. Chung's point is related by Lartey to Gerkin's elaborations of Boisen's image of the living human document.

My reflections in this chapter may seem to have carried us far from the car showroom in which I met Earl, who did not know what a rector is or does. Indeed, to remember Boisen is to remember a different time, and to focus on a hospital context quite different from Earl's world of auto sales. Yet the story of Anton Boisen is one of ministry beyond the church building, about presence far beyond the sanctuary. He was wrestling with questions about what a minister is and does, as one meeting perspectives like Earl's might in a later time and place. Boisen's own determination to find a place for ministry beyond congregational contexts also has much to do with questions of relevance, though they may be quite different from such questions as they now arise in our times and places. Nevertheless, the like of his anger at fleckless, untrained pastors drawing on inappropriate verses of scripture on hospital wards for the mentally distressed, and his own bold vision of the contribution and expertize of Christian ministers being brought to interdisciplinary work shared with colleagues in other disciplines, might inspire us to engagement with contemporary challenges and opportunities of ministry. Boisen's move into ministry beyond the sanctuary, if not in fully public space at least in the ambiguous space of psychiatric wards, can inspire contemporary ministers to find places in which to exercise care beyond the gatherings of the church. Indeed, Boisen's legacy has reformed the way in which ministry is understood, and theology is done, in many Christian traditions and in many parts of the world. His contribution to open, listening, collaborative, adjusting styles of theological reflection remains as vital now as it was then.

# CHAPTER 2

# Returning to the Word at Table: A Classical Tradition

A "classical" tradition regards itself as countercultural in the context of contemporary theological approaches that take interdisciplinary turns, toward therapy among other things. By contrast, it seeks to restore the priority of "theology" in pastoral theology—and in particular to find a role for classical theology, which means at least theology that is not tied so much to contemporary perspectives. So although the very title I have given this tradition suggests, being classical, that it relates to antique, early tradition, it *follows* the therapeutic tradition in this present ordering because in the context of the twentieth century it emerged subsequent to the therapeutic tradition, as a reaction to it. The basic charge that this tradition makes against the antecedent therapeutic tradition is that it is in fact in "therapeutic *captivity*"— that is, its theology is captive to therapy or other nontheological disciplines. (Another simple way of saying this is it views the therapeutic tradition as having "sold out" to therapeutic perspectives.) A classical approach to pastoral care, then, at the very least is likely to be suspicious of theological methods that give priority (temporal or theoretical) to other ("secular") disciplines. Indeed, some classical pastoral theology has been (sometimes self-) designated as "paleo-orthodox," that is, seeking a more ancient orthodoxy (so Thomas Oden, whom this chapter discusses).

## Essentials of Ministry

One important exponent of the classical tradition is Thomas C. Oden, an American ordained United Methodist theologian who in the early 1980s published two books around which the classical tradition was galvanized. In 1983, Oden published *Pastoral Theology: Essentials of Ministry* and a year later a book which gave further rise to this tradition, *Pastoral Care in the Classical Tradition*, and which has in its turn evoked further studies with similar titles.[1] What is so interesting about Oden is the way in which these books marked a conversion for him, in the sense that they show how he came to abandon some firmly held "liberal" theological convictions. Oden had been a student of Paul Tillich, formed in a liberal mentality, and had advocated for this tradition in a long series of prior publications. Through the 1980s, however, Oden carved out a second career in which he came to be clearly identified with evangelical expressions of Christianity, collating massive dictionaries of American evangelical biography and so assisting the fostering of memory in that particular tradition. As a paleo-orthodox theologian, Oden has gone on to provide lectionary companions that might introduce evangelical readers to patristic theological sources, and so on. The paleo-orthodox label and this particular kind of resourcing of evangelical tradition came later, for in *Pastoral Theology*, Oden calls his own position "ecumenically centrist,"[2] drawing on an understanding of Vincent of Lerin's maxim which affirms "what has been believed 'everywhere, always, and by all.' "

Oden's contribution is marked by a strong focus on the clergy, and an attempt to recover a classical sense of the role of clergypersons.

---

1. Notably Andrew Purves, *Pastoral Theology in the Classical Tradition* (Louisville: Westminster John Knox Press, 2001). See also Christopher A. Beeley, *Leading God's People: Wisdom from the Early Church for Today* (Grand Rapids, MI: Eerdmans, 2012).
2. Thomas Oden, *Pastoral Theology: Essentials of Ministry* (San Francisco, CA: HarperCollins, 1983), 10.

So *Pastoral Theology* opens with a verse of scripture, "Strike the shepherd, that the sheep may be scattered" (Zechariah 13:7), which already makes one of his key points: Classical expressions of Christian ministry related to shepherding had been lost under a welter of attention to psychological insight. Oden is concerned not only to correlate pastoral theology with the office, gifts, and function of the pastor[3] but to "sharpen anew the needed distinction" between ordained and lay, at least as he sees it.[4] He has faced considerable criticism for this, as well as for promoting a somewhat static view of the Christian tradition rather detached from contemporary experience: John Elford chastens, "There is no point in understanding the past if we have to abandon the present in order to do it."[5] Nevertheless, Oden sees his task as to recover the lost identity of pastoral care in a therapeutic milieu, resisting "psychologies accommodated cheaply into pastoral care without much self-conscious identity formation from the tradition."[6] He makes the point that classical approaches to pastoral care have rarely been *studied* since the 1920s when Boisen's approach rose to prominence. "Accommodation" is characteristic of the language he uses to make his charge[7] though this is important to underscore that he is not appealing for a wholesale ditching of the "best of modern psychotherapies,"[8] but rather making a firm insistence that such psychotherapies should not "define" pastoral work.[9] Part of this insistence is that pastoral care is wider than pastoral counseling, or indeed the work of any other helping "profession": because

---

3. Oden, *Pastoral Theology*, 311.

4. Oden, *Pastoral Theology*, 3.

5. John Elford, "A Response to Oden," in *Faith or Fear: A Reader in Pastoral Care and Counseling*, ed. Michael Jacobs (London: DLT, 1997), 21.

6. Thomas C. Oden, "Recovering Lost Identity," in Jacobs, *Faith or Fear*, 15.

7. Note repeated use of the notion of a "charge" in Oden's "Recovering Lost Identity." Presumably it is a play on his sense of the importance of a clearly defined ordination charge.

8. Oden, "Lost Identity," 16.

9. Oden, "Lost Identity," 16

the pastor/parishioner relation is . . . different than the usual relation that prevails between

> physician/patient
> teacher/student
> leader/follower
> attorney/client
> public official/citizen

all of these roles are in some sense analogous to various aspects of ministry, yet none encompasses ministry, because none accepts the full responsibility of soul care.[10]

Here, Oden wishes to draw on longstanding descriptors of the ordained as those entrusted with the weighty work of "the cure of souls." This means for him that, as opposed to other kinds of professional, "the pastor is more likely to compassionately behold the parishioner's whole existence—physical, moral, and spiritual—in the context of salvation history or universal history seen in relation to eternity."[11] One very important dimension of this relates to the unboundaried, "non-scheduled social format" of ministry[12] in which the pastor can always be creating opportunities to engage with and listen to others. Oden is emphatic that pastoral listening is different from gossip (that "repeat[s] bad news in a blaming, damaging way"), and that opportunities for listening must be related to a consistent engagement and demeanor among others which "open[s] up the wedge of possibility for significant encounters," and which empathic pastors are doing "even when it does not look like they are doing other things." So pastors are open to "serendipitous moments" in all kinds of happenchance circumstances, "whether between the acts of a school play or on a jogging track or after a tense committee meeting . . . at a backyard barbeque or after a funeral or over a second cup of morning coffee."

---

10. Oden, *Pastoral Theology*, 187.
11. Oden, *Pastoral Theology*, 187–88.
12. Oden, *Pastoral Theology*, 203. The following paragraph quotes from pages 202–3 of Oden's text.

Another major stress for Oden is the tradition of pastoral visitation to persons in their homes; and in particular visiting without specific request to do so: "The pastoral office carries with it the extraordinary privilege of calling upon persons in the parish at almost any time. This opens unparalleled opportunities for social service, intimate dialogue, and Christian witness."[13] He underlines that because this capacity and commission to make home visits is uninvited, "the non-scheduled social format is hardly at all like psychotherapy or legal service or business relationships—precisely because it is ministry."[14] Here then are perspectives and practices that Oden sees as essential to ordained ministry and that mark it out from the ways others may help persons. Within this context, Oden's reserve with pastoral counselling comes sharply into focus.

An early statement of intent identifies a number of further practices which he sees as marking a classical approach, and it is demanding in its range: intercessory prayer, resistance to antinomianism, recovery of traditional teaching on marriage, relating of empathy and the doctrine of incarnation, renewed emphasis on "*askesis*, self-discipline, self-denial" as these contribute to a healthy "Christian anthropology,"[15] moral self-examination in light of Bible studies and immersion in tradition, concern for the development of a pastoral theodicy, integration of witness into conversation, reappraisal of spiritual virtues and moral character, recovery of spiritual direction and counseling related to liturgy, preaching, and Christian community rather than "secularized, non-ecclesial, theologically emasculated fee basis counselling."[16] Evidently, at least by the point he had developed such a list, Oden was not enamored by the therapeutic tradition.

For the remainder of this chapter, we shall consider some particular features of classical pastoral care, elaborating themes in Oden's own work and expanding attention from Oden himself to others.

---

13. Oden, *Pastoral Theology*, 169.
14. Oden, *Pastoral Theology*, 203.
15. Oden, "Lost Identity," 17.
16. Oden, "Lost Identity," 17.

## Worship-Centered Care

### The Sunday Service[17]

At the head of Oden's list of "what clergy do and why" is worship-related activity. The classical tradition values the ways in which worship cares for persons. A very basic sense in which care can be offered is opportunity for worship being regularly, reliably made available, but beyond that, aspects of worship can be thought about in terms of the care of persons, and exponents of the classical tradition would suggest that pastors ought to be thinking about worship in this way. It is interesting, therefore, to reflect on the ecumenically affirmed shape of Christian assembly on Sunday, which now patterns eucharistic celebration across many different ecclesial traditions and church styles, in light of Oden's claims.[18] It involves praise, which is a practice of other-centeredness. Apart from anything else, praise requires the maturity of an excentric focus, partial and fragmentary as this will remain, as the practice of confession asserts in the very same Sunday service. The journey through the liturgy on Sundays also involves an invitation to repentance and ritualizes pathways through senses of guilt and shame. Nuanced as texts for Sunday confession are, and complemented as they are by related rites for other times and places, they provoke questions about opting for some measure of restoration and allege the availability of resources for reconciliation. The Sunday service also involves attention to Scripture, which is, amongst other things, a practice of engaging with the stories of diverse others. By listening to Moses cry and Miriam sing, to Jesus's silence as well as his words, and becoming immersed in the nuances of scriptural narratives, worshipers may

---

17. For more on this, see Stephen Burns, ed., *Journey* (Norwich: Canterbury Press, 2008).
18. See Thomas F. Best and Dagmar Heller, *Eucharistic Worship in Ecumenical Contexts: The Lima Liturgy—and Beyond* (Geneva: World Council of Churches, 1998), for the shape that is widely embraced across many ecclesial traditions, and Gordon W. Lathrop, *Holy Things: A Liturgical Theology* (Minneapolis, MN: Fortress Press, 1993) for key theological explorations of the shape. For recent discussion, see Stephen Burns, "A Fragile Future for the Ordo?" in *Worship and Culture: Foreign Country or Homeland?*, ed. Glaucia Vasconcelos Wilkey (Grand Rapids, MI: Eerdmans, 2014), 143–61.

become "mythically more"[19] than narrowly self-reflective narratives may allow. Much the same might be said about calendars of saints as patterns of access to variously challenging and resourceful others. Further, to suspect that "a world without saints forgets how to praise"[20] might be to begin to glimpse something of the mutually enriching interplay of liturgical practices.

The Sunday service also involves the demanding other-centered work of intercession. Ideally, such prayers of the people are structured so as to "reflect the wideness of God's mercy for the whole world."[21] Intercession is a key liturgical practice that can nurture compassion and ally compassion to action; at least "if for each thing we ask of God, the intent is our action in the world in God's name."[22] Then the Sunday service juxtaposes intercession with thanksgiving at table. Eucharistic praying is a practice that can cultivate habits of gratitude and evoke awareness of the dynamics of one's interactions with manifold others. Its invitation is to "receive what we are . . . [and] become what we receive./ **The body of Christ**."[23] Participation in the Eucharist is a central orienting activity of Christian assembly and yet may also orient activity beyond the assembly, if Don Saliers's views of the embodied actions of eucharistic prayer—taking, blessing, breaking, and giving bread and wine— are accepted as a pattern for Christian spirituality. Just as nourishment is shared, so the assembly "must be prepared to be given for others."[24] Congruence between text and environmental factors may be poignantly

---

19. See Gail Ramshaw, "Pried Open by Prayer," in *Liturgy and the Moral Self: Humanity at Full Stretch Before God: Essays in Honor of Don E. Saliers*, ed. E. Byron Anderson and Bruce T. Morrill, SJ (Collegeville, MN: Liturgical Press, 1998), 169–75.

20. Fred Pratt Green, "Rejoice in God's Saints," in *Together in Song: Australian Hymn Book II* (East Melbourne: HarperCollins, 1999), no. 470 (stanza 4).

21. Evangelical Lutheran Church in America, *Evangelical Lutheran Worship* (Minneapolis, MN: Augsburg Fortress Press, 2006), 105.

22. E. Bryon Anderson, "Linking Liturgy and Life," in *Worship Matters: A United Methodist Guide to Ways of Worship*, ed. E. Byron Anderson (Nashville, TN: Discipleship Resources, 1999), 1:68. See also Paul F. Bradshaw, *Two Ways of Praying: Introducing Liturgical Spirituality* (London: SPCK, 1995).

23. This dialogue is found in *Uniting in Worship 2* (Sydney: Uniting Church Press, 2005), 219.

24. Don E. Saliers, *Worship and Spirituality* (Akron, OH: OSL Publications, 1996), 67–68.

expressed in recovery of the *orant* posture (hands lifted in thanksgiving, and also stretched out, as if pinned to a cross) as a gesture for the whole assembly throughout eucharistic prayer, yielding the meaning attached to it in early explanations which stress its expression of both blessing and sacrifice, not one without the other.[25] The texts of eucharistic prayer are themselves careful to ensure that gratitude is articulated in close relation to a centripetal narrative of self-giving—that of Jesus. Gratitude may also be blended with lament: so a prayer from *Evangelical Lutheran Worship* addresses God as "God of our weary years, God of our silent tears" and calls out, "the cry of the poor has become your own cry; our hunger and thrdt for justice is your own desire." Then it praises this God for Jesus, who preached good news to the afflicted, broke bread with outcasts and those despised by others, and "ransom[ed] those in bondage to prejudice and sin."[26]

Finally, the Sunday service may well conclude with a word of mission that relates participation to responsibility beyond the assembly,[27] before closing with a purposeful dismissal: "Our worship is ended. **Our service begins**";[28] "Go in peace. Remember the poor. **In the name of Christ. Amen.**"[29] The ecumenically affirmed shape of Christian assembly on Sunday culminates in a "sending" which is always a summons to link liturgy and living beyond the assembly, to practice the grace for which the celebration is a school.

---

25. John K. Leonard and Nathan D. Mitchell, *The Postures of the Assembly During the Eucharistic Prayer* (Chicago, IL: Liturgy Training Publications, 1993) traces early practice; Richard Giles, *Creating Uncommon Worship: Transforming the Liturgy of the Eucharist* (Norwich: Canterbury Press, 2004), 159–80, seeks to retrieve this posture as a congregational, and not merely presidential, one.

26. *Evangelical Lutheran Worship*, 67.

27. An attractive feature of the Australian Uniting Church resources, interestingly mirrored in more recent editions of the Church of England's *Common Worship* range which have retrieved the "dismissal gospel" from the pre-conciliar Roman Catholic mass. See *Common Worship: Times and Seasons* (London: Church House Publishing, 2006).

28. Baptist Union of Great Britain, *Gathering for Worship: Patterns and Prayers for the Community of Disciples* (Norwich: Canterbury Press, 2005), 21 (bold case in original, indicating unison response).

29. *Evangelical Lutheran Worship*, 115 (bold case in original, indicating unison response).

## Other Sacraments

Oden's reflections on pastoral visitation suggest the development of such practice as a distinctively Protestant creative turn of Catholic practice of a particular sacrament. So he hints that classical approaches can also be developed through emphasis on liturgies of the life cycle, not just the directly dominical sacraments of baptism and Eucharist, but also of what Anglican tradition calls "common sacraments." If Christian assembly on Sundays is one cluster of practices, another is the seven sacraments, and Protestant appropriation of their Catholic practice. Indeed, one of Oden's contribution is to suggest certain lines of continuity between the seven sacraments of Catholic tradition and Protestant practices of pastoral care, which may have ditched the language of sacramentality but which continued to place stress and value at nodal points in the life cycle on which the sacraments focused. To begin to explore worship in such a way need not lead to a purely functional view of worship. The primacy of adoration is inherent in the praise with which Sundays and sacraments begin and which both sustain. Sundays and sacraments can be imagined as providing an ecology that is strongly hospitable to pastoral care; they offer a context in which pastoral care takes places—and not only that, but open up into a horizon of abundance, suggesting that human flourishing is the desire of the divine. Even so, this way of reflecting on worship must, as must every other way, be subject to some suspicion. Hurting persons will not necessarily, and certainly not instantly, be "healed" in worship. Thus ongoing scrutiny is required to prevent liturgical celebration collapsing into "eulogistic evasion."[30] Nevertheless, the classical tradition holds up high ideals for worship. Aspects of the service of the Lord's Day, and sacraments through the life cycle can each be means of offering care for persons in terms of ritualizing the possibility

---

30. This evocative phrase is Johann Baptist Metz's. For further applications to liturgy, see Bruce T. Morrill, SJ, *Anamnesis as Dangerous Memory: Political and Liturgical Theology in Dialogue* (Collegeville, MN: Liturgical Press, 2000) and Andrea Bieler and Luise Schottroff, *The Eucharist: Bodies, Bread and Resurrection* (Minneapolis, MN: Fortress Press, 2007).

of encounter with Christ, as though the pastoral caregiver herself stands aside to yield to Christ's own self-giving.

On various fronts, then, Oden's approach and elaborations on it offer sharp challenges to trajectories in the therapeutic tradition. As a classical approach might be developed, emphasis is squarely placed on what Gordon W. Lathrop calls the "central things," word and sacrament, which are perceived (indeed, "received") as means of gracious divine self-revelation. Derivatively, any attempt to foster a sense of the sacramental might be regarded as part of a classical approach.

## "Walking Sacraments"

Not all exponents of the classical tradition would wish to follow Oden in distinguishing so sharply lay and ordained pastoral caregivers, but they are likely to hold ordained ministry in esteem. Hence, thinking about ordination, and about ordained ministries among other ministries, is likely to be important. One way of discussing ordained ministry is in relation to the notion of "walking sacraments." Austin Farrer's famous sermon with that name is a remarkable reflection on ordained ministry, preached at a priest's first mass as presiding celebrant. Farrer locates the "essentials" and "distinctive place" of priestly ministry at the altar table, where "he sets forth the mystery of love, the body and blood of Christ, in bread and wine."[31] Farrer identifies the particular contribution of ordained persons in a very simple correlation with divine presence in sacramental celebration:

> You know what is the special mercy of Christ to us in the Sacraments. It is, that he just puts himself there. He does not make it depend on anything special in us who receive, certainly not in anything special in the bread and wine; not in anything special in the priest either, except just that he is a priest.

---

31. Austin Farrer, "Walking Sacraments," in *The Truth-Seeking Heart: Austin Farrer and His Writings*, ed. Ann Loades and Robert MacSwain (Norwich: Canterbury Press, 2006), 139. The following paragraphs quote from pages 139–41 of Farrer's sermon.

Here, Farrer proposes a notion of the priest acting—albeit momentarily—*in persona Christi*, but more importantly suggests that a priest is *always* "a sort of walking sacrament." God speaks "from over the priest's shoulders." Notably, however, he is adamantly nonhierarchical in his stress that the priest is in no way better than any one else:

> Anyone may be a better Christian than the priest, more holy in life, more versed in prayer. But the priest has a special obligation to lead a devout life, to study divinity, to pray; and so to be fit to give some help to his fellow-Christians in these supremely important concerns. Other people may expound the faith, and speak or write in Christ's name, more wisely and more competently than the priest. They *may* do such things, and even do them better; but the priest *must*; he must keep the congregation supplied with its staple diet: he must keep giving them some word from God.

Farrer is also quick to point out that in a certain sense all Christians act at times *in persona Christi*: as he says, "none of us can be let off being Christ in our place and our station: we are all pigmies in giants' armor." He sees this responsibility, shared by all Christians, lay and ordained, as "the price we pay for the mercy of God," "that he does not wait for our dignity or perfection, but just puts himself there in our midst; in the bread and this wine: in this priest: in this Christian man, woman, or child":

> He who gave himself to us first as an infant, crying in a cot, he who was hung up naked on the wood, does not stand on our dignity. If Jesus is willing to be in us, and to let us show him to the world, it's a small thing that we should endure being fools for Christ's sake, and be shown up by the part we have to play.

## The Company of the Saints

Times and seasons of the liturgical calendar might also play their part in the environment in worship, alongside scripture, sacraments, and the particular gift of ordained ministry, in mediating pastoral care. In particular the churches' calendars of saints can be a resource for encouraging engagement with the durable divine gifts of word and sacrament. Certainly Oden invites renewed attention to the spiritual classics of the Christian tradition, yielded to contemporary readers from many different times and places, and many of which were written by those who are now honored as saints. The *sanctorales* of different churches have different weight and different meanings; nevertheless, many different traditions honor the same persons, one of whom is Gregory the Great, the author of an early and durable treatise on pastoral care.

### Gregory the Great

Classical or "paleo-orthodox" pastoral theologians draw on numerous ancient sources, but perhaps above all Gregory the Great's treatise. Gregory was the first monk to be made pope. He has been described as "Europe's greatest reformer, perhaps excepting Luther,"[32] and by any reckoning has exercised enormous influence on European culture and Christian spirituality, theology, and ministry.

In 597 Gregory sent Anselm of Canterbury as missionary to the British Isles and so is in a sense responsible for the mediation of the Christian tradition to those islands and those to whom missionaries from England themselves came many years later. Gregory is best known for his *Pastoral Rule*, but he also wrote numerous biblical commentaries, books on Italian saints, including Benedict. He famously described himself as "servant of the servants of God" and equally famously fondly echoed Gregory of Nazianzus's description of pastoral care as the "art of arts." The rule was read in different Mediterranean regions even in Gregory's lifetime, and after his death only grew in influence. His rule is in four parts: The first is about the burdens of leadership and necessary qualities in those who take up leadership; the second treats the pastor's life and conduct, and is concerned with the typically monastic tension between contemplation and action; the third relates to preaching to different people; the fourth is about "returning to oneself" through thinking

---

32. Philip Culbertson and Arthur Bradford Shippee, eds., *The Pastor: Readings from the Patristic Period* (Minneapolis, MN: Fortress Press, 1990), 187.

about one's own weaknesses in order to avoid a sinful sense of self-infla-tion. The artist of all arts needs, in Gregory's estimation, more skill than even a physician. So great learning is needed to be a pastoral caregiver, and people are not fit to undertake pastoral care without deep thought and study. But there is more than that: What is learned must be lived—"no one does more harm in the Church than he who has the title or rank of holiness and acts perversely" (1.2).[33] There is a necessary unworldli-ness about pastoral caregivers—they reject the esteem and accolades that others may chase. Pastors have a constant need to undertake self-examination, so as not to fall into sin, yet must constantly risk distraction: They must not live interior lives, or even lives of deep communion with God that exclude others—for just as Christ the only begotten Son of God "came forth from the bosom of the Father into our midst so that he might benefit the many" (1.5) so the pastor must be focused on others. Of the many qualities required of pastors, prayer is the most important, however (1.10), and intercession the basis for all pastoral encounter.

Gregory's rule has higher expectations of pastors than of other Christians—in this sense, his is not an egalitarian vision (indeed, Gregory speaks most often of the pastor as "rector," ruler), however insistent that Gregory may be about pastors constantly remembering their own sinful-ness so as not to think highly of themselves. Pastors are to be committed to the highest aspirations in their speech, conduct, discernment, compas-sion, contemplation, humility, and zeal. There are to be no half measures in the pastor's reception of grace, and the pastor's response to grace is to be made in word and deed. The pastor's response to grace is also to express, deeply, both contemplation of God and action toward neigh-bors; indeed, great intimacy with both God and people. Their words and deeds are to evoke from people a willingness to reveal themselves to the pastor "as a crying child seeks its mother's breast" (2.5). Pastors are also to be attentive to the physical needs of people—their care is to be fully rounded, not simply focused on "the spiritual." Food for the poor and mediating with armies are both appropriate concerns.

---

33. In this section, references to Gregory's text are given in brackets after each extract.

Contemporary readers might not always affirm Gregory's hierarchies or feel comfortable with all his concerns, but there is undeniably a sensitivity and insightfulness in Gregory. While Gregory warns about the consequences of sin, his main thrust is not threat, but encouragement to beckon grace, to take the "medicine" God offers to make human persons well.

Gregory also distinguishes between public and more personal encounters with people—so when preaching, the pastor cannot be as direct as he might be in pastoral conversation: In preaching "the greatest good should be praised in a way that does not ignore lesser goods" (3.36), and he may need to focus on encouraging people to abandon major sins even if and when this means they continue in minor sins. There is a kind of gradualism in this that recognizes that people can cope with one thing at a time. But above all, the pastor is to be aware that his deeds in life speak louder than his words: His "flock" needs to be able to follow the footprints of the pastor's actions, not just the sound of the pastor's voice!

Finally, Gregory presses home the importance of the pastor's willingness for self-examination and reflection. He ends by asking his imaginary reader ("John"), to whom the rule is addressed, to pray for him as someone who has written to direct others to "the shores of perfection" even though he himself is "shipwrecked by sin."

### George Herbert

George Herbert (1593–1633) is well-known as one of the greatest English poets, famous for his corpus of poems, *The Temple: Sacred Poems and Private Ejaculations*, which includes the like of his Love III: "Love bade me welcome," of which Gordon Mursell suggests that there may have been "no more subtle, more economical, more sheerly attractive, presentation of the epicenter of Protestant spirituality."[34]

In addition to his poetry, Herbert also produced a practical manual on pastoral ministry, which was the first of its kind to be written in

---

34. Gordon Mursell, *English Spirituality* (London: SPCK, 2001), 1:437.

English. In *The Country Parson*, Herbert initiated a genre that spawned imitators, among which is Richard Baxter's equally famous *The Reformed Pastor*, and which is clearly indebted to *The Country Parson*, appearing four years later than Herbert's work. Herbert was also a contemporary of the English religious poet John Donne (1572–1631) and his lifetime overlapped with the spiritual odysseys—the pilgrim's progress—of John Bunyan (1628–88). Herbert wrote *The Country Parson* as rector of Fuggleton-with-Bremerton, two tiny villages on the edge of Salisbury in the southwest of England. He occupied that role for the last three years of his life, after an earlier career in both academia and politics. Certainly, his poetry reflects many dimensions of interior struggle, with a recurring sense of "soure-sweet" response to divine calling upon his life:

> I will complain, yet praise,
> I will bewail, approve,
> And all my soure-sweet days
> I will lament, and love ("Bitter-sweet").[35]

Herbert held preaching—and particularly biblically based preaching —in high esteem, yet prayer was of higher importance to him: "Resort to sermons, but to prayer most / praying's the end of preaching" (his poem, "The Church Porch"). His manual is given in parts to encourage diligence in preparation for worship and of the environment of prayer, including care for buildings and furnishings (CP, chs. 6, 13). For example, "at great festivalls [the church building is to be] strawed, and stuck with boughs, and perfumed with incense," and at all times to have gravity, with no "foolish anticks" (CP, ch. 13). According to one famous anecdote from his life, shortly after taking up the parish in Bremerton, he was discovered lying prostrate in prayer before the altar in the village church.

Moreover, his prayer is not simply a solitary experience, however often or not he may have lain prostrate in an empty church. For Herbert, public prayer has "more promises, more love" than its private expression.

---

35. In this section, references to Herbert's texts are given in brackets after each extract. Poetry is in the public domain.

And so with the word and prayer, the sacraments were of prime importance to Herbert. He called the Eucharist a "feaste of Charity" and it was
for him an awesome event: "Especially at communion time [the country
parson] is in great confusion, as being not only to receive God, but to
break and administer him" (CP, ch. 22).

The pastor is seen as both "Deputy for Christ" (CP, ch. 2), perhaps especially in sacramental celebration, and as representative of the
church. The pastor's representative role comes into focus in the event of
worship, which is to be led "as being truly touched and amazed with the
Majesty of God, before whom [the pastor] then presents himself; yet not
as himself alone, but as presenting with himself the whole Congregation"
(CP, ch. 6). Herbert's manual revolves around the central things of word
and sacrament, and his is a thoroughgoing ecclesial approach to pastoral
care. Another of his best-loved poems, "Aaron," depicts his own awareness of personal frailty, but confidence to serve on the basis of Christ's
presence in him:

> Holiness on the head,
> Light and perfection on the breast,
> Harmonious bells below, raising the dead
> To lead them unto life and rest:
> Thus are true Aarons dressed.
>
> Profaneness in my head,
> Defects and darkness in my breast,
> A noise of passions ringing me for dead
> Unto a place where is no rest:
> Poor priest thus am I dressed.
>
> Only another head
> I have, another heart and breast,
> Another music, making live not dead,
> Without whom I could have no rest:
> In him I am well dressed.
>
> Christ is my only head,
> My alone only heart and breast,

My only music, striking me ev'n dead,
That to the old man I may rest,
And be in him new dressed.

So holy in my head,
Perfect and light in my dear breast,
My doctrine tuned by Christ (who is not dead,
But lives in me while I do rest),
Come people, Aaron's dressed.

Yet while conscious of own priestly role, in another and important sense he regarded the vocation of the whole of humankind as priestly: "Man is the world's high Priest," he declares in his poem of praise, "Providence."

*The Country Parson* consists of thirty-seven chapters and two prayers (for use before and after preaching). Herbert describes his own purpose in writing it thus: "I have resolved to set down the form and character of a true pastor, that I may have a mark to aim at" (the Preface of the edition published in 1632). He saw what he had written as being incomplete, but as something that could "grow into" a complete pastoral guide. The range of activities he did take in view from his central attention to word and sacrament is quite remarkable. For example, with preaching, catechizing is seen as an important part of the pastor's role (CP, ch. 21), and Herbert is adamant not only that "the parson's library is a holy life" (CP, ch. 33) but that the preacher's life is "it selfe a sermon." He depicts the pastor as one with whom spiritual conversation runs through all encounters and activities, not only at church, but when visiting, and when offering hospitality to others in their own home. The hospitality of the pastor's own home is important, and moreover, it is important to invite all to the parsonage, without favoritism. A range of pastoral practices are commended, including "particular confession" (CP, ch. 15), the sacrament of penance, for those who would benefit from it, and a great interest in healing. Herbert suggests that the pastor might himself learn to apply the healing properties of herbs, though they are only to be applied with prayer—to "raise the action from the shop to the church"—as well as keeping a physician in the household, or else developing a close relationship with local physicians if neither the pastor nor the pastor's spouse is a healer (CP, ch. 10). In any case, it is a pastor's work to ensure basic care of the body, as part of the "completeness" (CP, ch. 23) of ministry. The completeness of the pastor's work also means that, as well as physician, he might need to act as a lawyer, arbitrating; and Herbert is adamant that he also needs to know something of agriculture, out of respect for local knowledge and custom. He regards this local knowledge as essential for the pastor to take up the home visiting Herbert encourages pastors to conduct each weekday afternoon. To face what he may encounter on his rounds of visiting, the pastor must "digest all the points of consolation" which includes consolation to overcome distraction in prayer.

Perhaps not everything Herbert had to say about "country people" was entirely respectful. It is not only that they may need stories and sayings more than abstract ideas from their pastor (CP, ch. 7), it is that "country people . . . are thick, and heavy, and hard to raise to the point of Zeal" (Sermon 2:13). Nevertheless, pastors are encouraged to attend to the details of their parishioners' lives: They must "carry their eyes ever open, and fix them on their charge" (CP, ch. 26). And with that encouragement comes a cutting-down-to-size of those who might seek to minister to the "thick" country folk. Simply by "dwelling in their bookes, [scholarly clergy] will never finde" some of what they need for ministry (CP, ch. 26). And alongside their prayer and their preaching, to be witnessed in the personal encounter enabled by visiting, perhaps, the most compelling thing they can offer to others is the witness of their holiness, manifest in their own "rejoicing in another's good"—the greatest sign of sanctity (CP, ch. 6).

While no doubt some aspects of Herbert's legacy do not "translate" to contemporary contexts in any easy way, much might yet be appreciated. Gordon Mursell suggests that Herbert's interest is primarily in "the way we experience God's saving work in us."[36] As he expands: "Few (perhaps no) others have explored the question of what might constitute

---

36. Gordon Mursell, *The Story of Christian Spirituality: East and West, Two Thousand Years* (London: Lion, 2001), 258.

'spiritual life' for a devout Protestant with anything like the sharpness and breadth of vision"[37] of Herbert. There can, therefore, be no rigid distinction between pastoral care and spirituality. This point is one that challenges not only ways in which "pastoral" action may be detached from spiritual traditions in some contemporary practice, but also some strands in ways that, say, the therapeutic tradition has developed, which while in one sense searching for "holistic" integration of psychological and theological insight might in another sense neglect full attention to spiritual practice, at least in its communal, embodied, and ecclesial dimensions. Pastoral care is centrally concerned with formation in spirituality, in public worship, and in personal prayer; it has aesthetic, and not only rational, aspects; and it encourages a kind of all-embracing, non-compartmentalization of life. Herbert's country parson, like Gregory's pastor, is a fine exponent of the classical tradition of pastoral theology, and they each represent the kind of wisdom that Oden and others wish to make more central to the practice of pastoral care.

Just as was said of Boisen at the close of the previous chapter, to remember figures who have been the focus of this chapter is also to remember times and places quite different from many contemporary contexts of ministry. Gregory and Herbert are long gone leaders, and to valorize them uncritically may prove profoundly unhelpful to modern-day ministers.[38] What may be helpful to remember, though, is that neither Herbert nor Gregory see the pastor's task as exclusively oriented to "spiritual" matters: Gregory insists that pastors meet the physical need of others, from mediating with warring forces to feeding the poor. Ministry is not confined to the sanctuary or just spiritual matters. And alongside Herbert's legacy to Anglican hymnody, we might also recall his call for wide hospitality, concern for healing, and cooperation with physicians.

---

37. Mursell, *English Spirituality*, 1:424.
38. A point well made in Justin Lewis-Anthony, *If You Meet George Herbert on the Road, Kill Him: Radically Re-thinking Pastoral Ministry* (London: Mowbray, 2009).

Herbert might have a focus on what we could call sacramental ministry, but its context is what he himself calls the completeness of ministry. The altar table of the church stands at the nexus of something much more wide-ranging.

It is this understanding of the completeness of care that I relate to my opening vignette about the space around me on a crowded train as I wore a clerical collar. What both Gregory and Herbert can still help even contemporary ministers think through is some aspects of what they do as crucial to their Christian identity, and what Oden calls "essentials" of ministry. What might be considered essential is that ministry does its best to point to Christ, with whom prejudice and abuse are not welcome. So even after centuries Gregory and Herbert raise questions about what the mediation of Christ involves, the congruence of the pastor's enactment with the word she or he proclaims, his or her doctrine in tune with ("tuned to") Christ.

In his own recollection of "classical" patterns of ministry, Oden was no doubt in contest with some of what Boisen stood for. There is not enough word and table in the therapeutic tradition for his liking. But the options for our contemporary alliances are not simply between Boisen and Oden, who might be perceived as marking one polarity or another, one perhaps too far away from a sense of Christian distinctiveness, the other too preoccupied with the heritage of the past rather than communication with and relevance to the present. In the prejudice and abuse in the church of which contemporary persons are all too aware, it is the association of the symbols of ministry with the beauty of Christ that is under threat at the present time, the link between the church and the gospel that is tenuous. Into this dilemma, the classical tradition asserts the importance of reference to Christ, while the therapeutic tradition resources the means of listening and engagement with others. Both are crucial in ministry. Farrer, for his part, reminds us of the messiness of "being there" for others in faithfulness to Christ, and that may be the very least of what needs to be understood when wondering how to relate to Earl and his kind, seemingly with no clues about what a rector is, or to what Christian ministry refers or offers.

# CHAPTER 3

# Erecting Streetlights on the Road to Jericho: A Liberationist Tradition

The liberationist tradition of pastoral care is both a response to the preceding styles of care and also especially indebted to liberation theologies. It is concerned to see care widely and holistically related to the contexts in which people live as much as their inner or spiritual lives understood more narrowly. Specifically, it regards the therapeutic tradition as "captive" to therapeutic emphases, although its concern is not so much that of the classical tradition—that the therapeutic style is not sufficiently related to scripture and "classics" of the tradition. Rather, the problem as the liberationist tradition perceives it is that the therapeutic tradition is too individualistic. It adopts too narrow a view of care that fails to see individuals in their social context, their network of relationships. Consequently, the healing it offers may result simply in adjusting persons to their environments, rather than recognizing that the environments themselves may need to be changed. This point can then be elaborated in ways that both ally and distance it from the classical tradition. As the classical tradition critiques the therapeutic tradition—viewing it is insufficiently intertwined with the Christian heritage—the liberationist tradition likewise offers critique to the classical tradition for too easily emphasizing a kind of spirituality which is not now robust enough in relation to its cultural surroundings. It too, then, may simply adjust persons—making them better Bible readers or contemplatives, more participative in liturgy, perhaps—but nevertheless incapable of challenging their environments.

Even so, the liberationist tradition does share emphases with the two traditions considered previously. In the first place, it emphatically underlines the starting place of pastoral theology in human experience and so stands in at least a certain continuity with the work of Anton Boisen. Indeed, the therapeutic tradition has itself evolved in self-critical style, with those who have followed Boisen both suggesting their dependence on him and widening his emphasis. The notion of the "living human web" recontextualizes Boisen's "living human document," and will be further explored in the present chapter. As Bonnie Miller-McLemore developed the image of the web, she was particularly indebted to feminist perspectives. Others in the liberation tradition have been as likely to take their lights from the methodologies that have been popularized in liberation theology, both directly and in the forms that have influenced methodology in feminist theology.

## Liberation Theology as Contextual Theology

Liberation theologians have shaped all subsequent contextual theologies in so far as they have all come to share its emphatic insistence that the starting place of theology is its context. Indeed, liberation theology can be regarded as one of the geneses of contextual theology.[1] It is, however, marked by a distinctive and abiding commitment to add to others' contextual concern for "relevance" further concerns about justice and equity.

As a contextual theology, liberation theology takes its themes from the situations in which it develops, and so does not usually begin from "a conventional academic syllabus" by considering items on the systematic

---

1. Charles H. Kraft, "Contextual Theology," in *Dictionary of Pastoral Care and Counseling,* ed. Rodney Hunter et al. (Nashville, TN: Abingdon, 1991), 604.

agenda: God, Christ, salvation, church, sacraments, and so on.[2] Rather, it begins and proceeds by attending to context through listening to those who inhabit a particular environment—hence the importance of testimony, understood very broadly, and perhaps in alliance with notions like that of reading "living human documents."

In addition to testimony, gathering perspectives from the social sciences is also important to a great deal of contextual theology. Much controversy has occurred around some liberation theologies' appropriations of Marxist social and economic theory. Whatever might be made of that particular alliance, it should be noted that the interdisciplinary nature of such engagements suggest another potential commonality with the therapeutic tradition. The descriptive and analytic value of social science material is highly prized as it is in turn brought into dialogue with more traditional sources in theological construction: scripture and commentators upon it, representative figures in the Christian traditions, texts, and practice in liturgy, et cetera.

Hence, given the importance of such dialogue and its developments, contextual theology is best understood as a related "family" of theologies rather than as one single entity. Gustavo Gutierrez's *A Theology of Liberation* and Rosemary Radford Ruether's *Sexism and God-talk* are among the most influential writings from the "elders" in the "family." Theologies of mission have also been strong players in the development of contextual theological approaches: Vincent Donovan's *Christianity Rediscovered: An Epistle from the Masai*[3] on his experience of missionary work among an African people is widely regarded as an early contemporary "classic" of contextual theology. *All* theology, preceding it or contemporaneous with the recent emergence of a distinct discipline of contextual theology is indeed also contextual. What this means is that every theologian is affected by her "blood" and "bread"—blood: family,

---

2. Archbishop of Canterbury's Commission on Urban Priority Areas, *Faith in the City* (London: Church House Publishing, 1985), 67.
3. Vincent Donovan, *Christianity Rediscovered: An Epistle from the Masai* (London: SCM Press, 1982).

race, gender, sexuality, psychology; bread: location, livelihood, dependencies, socioeconomic status, and so on.[4] John Vincent makes the point:

> All theology is, and has always been, contextual. All theology is
> done in the first place by listening to the questions that arise for
> people, and those questions are determined by their contexts.
> Even and especially theologies that come to us as dogmatic were
> created originally within and by their contexts.[5]

Since Gustavo Gutierrez's classic *Theology of Liberation*, first published in 1971, liberation theologians have consistently stated that theology itself is "a second act, a turning back, a reflecting, that comes after
action." Theology is "not first . . . it arrives later on," following analysis of
a particular situation.

Feminist theology, which might minimally be defined as "a movement that seeks change for the better for women,"[6] may begin with a
similarly committed stance: the recognition that, apart from both massive disparities in opportunity and injustices in what is for many the
"privileged West," human life in large parts of Asia and North Africa suf-
fers from a persistent failure to give girls and women medical care, food,
or access to social services similar to that which men receive. Together,
this amounts to the charge that "sexism is not something that hurts
women's feelings, sexism is something that kills millions and millions of
girls and women each year."[7]

In the case of both liberation and feminist theology, explicitly theological reflection is "bracketed out" of the first stage of the process of
reflection upon particular situations, as the first stage is occupied with
acknowledgement of a situation, albeit in its sometimes profound horror.

---

4. John Vincent, "An Urban Hearing for the Church," in *Gospel from the City*, ed. John
Vincent and Chris Rowland (Sheffield: Urban Theology Unit, 1999), 115. See also John
Vincent, "Developing Contextual Theologies," *Epworth Review* 27 (2000): 62–77.
5. John Vincent, "Liberation Theology in Britain 1975–1995," in *Liberation Theology UK*,
ed. John Vincent and Christopher Rowland (Sheffield: Urban Theology Unit, 1995), 18.
6. Ann Loades, ed., *Feminist Theology: A Reader* (London: SPCK, 1990), 1.
7. Janet Martin Soskice, "Just Women's Problems?" in *Spiritual Classics from the Late
Twentieth Century*, ed. Ann Loades (London: Church House Publishing, 1994), 55.

A related method is now also familiar in articulate forms of pastoral theology—for example, as we saw in an earlier chapter in John Patton's book, *From Ministry to Theology: Pastoral Action and Reflection* (the title of which conveys the order of shifts in attention: "from . . . to, action . . . reflection"[8]).

## Bandages or Streetlights?

A powerful version of the liberation tradition emerged in places where pastoral ministry is less tied than in other places to pastoral counseling, but rather has been more broad based, finding its place in a context in which church and state are related in historic ways, the legacy of which is an opportunity for the churches' ministries.[9] In Britain, a champion of the liberation approach is Stephen Pattison, who prior to becoming a teacher of theology at Birmingham University had been a psychiatric nurse and a parish priest. From a post in pastoral theology at Birmingham, he moved to interdisciplinary posts with the Open University, where his work covered the like of "secular" management culture and the culture of the National Health Service. He has subsequently returned to Birmingham, to a post as chair in ethics, religion, and society. Even from these brief notes on his career trajectory, it is clear that his interests have been wide.

In his argument about "politics and pastoral care," Pattison challenges the view that the individual should be central to pastoral care, as "many of the things which affect the well-being of individuals for good or ill originate in the social and political order."[10] This recognition is not always common, however, which Pattison ascribes to a number of factors, including an emphasis on counseling and psychotherapy in pastoral care—a critique of the therapeutic tradition and the pervasiveness

---

8. John Patton, *From Ministry to Theology: Pastoral Action and Reflection* (Nashville, TN: Abingdon Press, 1990).
9. Note the important critique of Bonnie Miller McLemore, ed., *The Wiley-Blackwell Companion to Practical Theology* in Eric Stoddart, *Advancing Practical Theology: Critical Discipleship for Disturbing Times* (London: SCM Press, 2014), 108–19.
10. Stephen Pattison, *A Critique of Pastoral Care* (London: SCM Press, 1993), 82.

of individualistic approaches to religion and theology that find their place in the individualistic trends of wider Western societies. Further, processes of secularization may suggest to pastors that their capacity to influence wider circles is decreasing, so that pastors abandon the attempt to engage wider social structures and content themselves with ministry to individuals. As Pattison claims, "Pastoral care which concentrates on individuals, especially if it is informed by the insights of psychology and pastoral counselling, may be a way some pastors find meaning and a role in a world which does not seem to want them."[11] Finally, the adoption of professional role models by pastors has played a part, coalescing with the sense that religion is a private matter. Aspects of the pastoral care traditions themselves, when not held in tension with other aspects, provide elements that within these dynamics can be unhelpfully enlarged in individualistic approaches to care: Confession to a priest in the Catholic tradition is cited as an example.

Contrary to these trends, however, Pattison makes a case for sociopolitical action as a key part of pastoral care. He asserts that not only is an individualistic approach a misrepresentation of the practice of pastoral care, and indeed, traditional approaches to it, but that all pastoral care has social and political implications, and that sometimes acting in terms of these implications is crucial. He draws on notions of the human person as a holistic entity, and he pushes this holistic approach to suggest that pastoral care fosters "liberating wholeness" enabling persons to develop into their full human potential. He also picks up theological arguments that resist the division of "public" and "private" realms, insisting instead that persons are "at all times" bound up with social and political groupings. Furthermore, persons' actual experience of pastoral care oftentimes does seem to suggest that they can discover that "faith and vulnerability are possible."[12] Indeed, the very point of pastoral care is to form communities that respond to the needs of the world. Elements in the traditions of pastoral care are read as confirming this conviction. In Hebrew scripture, for example, pastoral imagery is applied to monarchs,

---

11. Pattison, *Critique*, 86.
12. Pattison, *Critique*, 91.

and pastoral language has clear corporate and public dimensions. In the New Testament, Jesus's healing ministry had clear communal dimensions and his preaching of the divine reign was not simply in individualistic terms. In view of these arguments, Pattison poses a range of apt questions for pastors:

> Who has power in a particular context? How is that power to be used and to what ends? What are the values being served and who benefits and in what way from the way things are? These are essential ethical questions.[13]

Unless pastoral care faces such questions, despite its possible claim to neutrality, it has inevitably become partisan, inhibiting the possibility of reconciliation by settling for conciliation: a shallow peace achieved by the domination of some by others, with injustice intact. To dislodge this kind of "peacefulness," "open conflict" may be necessary, and pastors may have a part to play in it.

To engage the sociopolitical context of care, Pattison promotes both use of the social sciences and active listening to people speaking for themselves about their experience—an emphasis directly absorbed from liberation theologians. Here once more Pattison appeals for revision of notions of reconciliation that clearly delineate it from conciliation, the latter being "cooling out opposition, adjusting people to oppression, and disguising the fact that injustice is rife."[14] Identifying what he sees as the space between conciliation and reconciliation, Pattison affirms, "Liberation . . . has to take place before reconciliation of the two sides is possible—without liberation there is not reconciliation but conciliation."[15]

## The Living Human Web

If Pattison represents a particular kind of fusion of pastoral and liberationist perspectives, Bonnie Miller-McLemore has been champion of

---

13. Pattison, *Critique*, 100–101.

14. Stephen Pattison, *Pastoral Care and Liberation Theology* (Cambridge: Cambridge University Press, 1993), 225.

15. Pattison, *Liberation Theology*, 225.

a distinctive feminist development. In particular, she has offered the image of "the living human web" both to complement and correct Boisen's earlier concern to read "documents." She is professor of pastoral theology at Vanderbilt University, a United Methodist–related school in Tennessee, USA, and is an ordained minister of the Church of Christ (Disciples). She wrote her first feminist essay on "the living human web" before singly authored books by women had been published in pastoral theology. Miller-McLemore's work on the living human web has evolved in a number of journal articles over time.[16] Her assessment of Boisen has combined both critique and appreciation, fused in her emphasis on the "living human document within the web." While affirming Boisen's "powerful foundation metaphor," her arguments contest "care narrowly defined as counseling,"[17] insisting that individuals always need to be understood—and cared for—"as part of a wide cultural, social, and religious context." She has Boisen, among others, in her sights for conceiving of care in terms of individuals, no matter how much interdisciplinarity they may seek. What approaches like Boisen's and others' need is more "social analysis of oppression and alienation, exploitation, diversity and justice in its clinical assessment of individual pathology." Crucially, analysis of contexts, "partially fostered by liberation perspectives," is critical if notions of pastoral care are "to be taken seriously by people of color and by white women." Miller-McLemore is herself a white woman, but she evidently sees her feminist arguments as enmeshed with a range of other perspectives from the "underside."

Her talk of structures and ideologies links to her central metaphor of the web. Miller-McLemore sees it as evoking the "dense, multitudinous, contiguous nature of reality," which might well resonate with process theology perspectives as well as being able to draw on a body of feminist literature already employing the metaphor. While feminist

---

16. Some collected in Bonnie Miller-McLemore, *Christian Theology in Practice: Discovering a Discipline* (Grand Rapids, MI: Eerdmans, 2012).
17. Bonnie Miller-McClemore, "The Living Human Web," in *Images of Pastoral Care: Classic Readings*, ed. Robert C. Dykstra (Cleveland, OH: Chalice Press, 2004), 41. The following paragraph's quote from pages 41–45 of Miller-McClemore's essay.

perspectives have sometimes explored the metaphor of the web as an image of interconnectedness, Miller-McLemore also draws attention to a more difficult dynamic. Citing Catherine Keller's work that explores the metaphor of the web evoking fear of enmeshment, entanglement, and loss, she recognizes that patriarchal thinking has often been reserved about the image.

As she wishes to develop the metaphor herself, a "web" of care would connect concern for individuals to social and political practice, so "public policy issues that determine the health of the human web are as important as issues of individual emotional well-being." In pushing for such a wider perspective, Miller-McLemore does not, however, abandon a sense of the importance of the more psychologically orientated emphasis of Boisen and of those who followed him. For while wishing to draw more explicitly on the interpretive insight of other social sciences alongside psychology—"psychology alone cannot understand the web"—she also wishes to see the discipline of psychology itself subject to ongoing feminist scrutiny. As it is, the effect of psychology that is not sensitized to feminist perspectives combines with patriarchal theologies in too many modes of pastoral care in which women—with black and Asian persons—are habitually seen as "others": the recipients of care rather than agents of it. Miller-McLemore cites an example of such "othering" in the effort to empathize with the cultural situation of the care seeker. Often, she suggests, women of color who are "othered" by patriarchal ways of seeing the world are habitually required to exercise something like "interempathy" so as to be able to relate to more dominant (white) male perspectives. In a turn characteristic of liberation theology, she therefore proposes that the "first step of those in second cultures is to affirm their own realities as worthy of equal respect." It is one thing for persons from dominant cultures to empathize with those of a second culture, but subordinated persons *must* do so all the time. Pastoral care needs to become more savvy about such dynamics. Furthermore, she asserts that some men are unable to develop sufficient empathy to be appropriate caregivers of women, that is, they are incapable of making a shared exploration of women's experience of pain, anger, and struggle. "The problem may not be too little empathy but too much indiscriminate empathy of an uninformed pastoral care." In various ways, then, male pastoral caregivers are challenged to sharpen their sensitivities—again not only to psychological aspects of women's experience but also to socioeconomic and political ones. And the discipline of pastoral theology in which male perspectives have remained prominent—in part because it is obviously linked with practices of Christian ministry, which are sometimes still restricted by churches to their male members—must likewise raise its game. Once more, in a turn characteristic of liberation theologies, Miller-McLemore insists that this will mean listening to people, especially women, as they speak for themselves. Pastoral theology and pastoral care cannot simply be male "readings" of women's experience. Moreover, "a web cannot be read like a document."

As Miller-McLemore's work on the living human web has developed over time, she has come to stress "the living document within the web." This has involved surfacing appreciation of Boisen's contribution that had gone unnoted in her earlier work. Latterly, she has affirmed Boisen's efforts to respond to the distance between theology and practice in pastoral ministry, and has reassessed Boisen as revolutionizing Protestant theological education. Part of her emerging appreciation of Boisen is a response to developing criticism in the discipline of pastoral theology of a "clerical paradigm" of care. In this paradigm, care is overly confined to clergy to the detriment of the ministry of whole people of God. Miller-McLemore, however, also names another problem, what she calls an "academic paradigm" which threatens to open up the distance from practice that Boisen sought to close. As she sees it, too much academic pastoral theology has been particularly misled and "obscured by captivation with diagnosis of" the clerical paradigm, creating an at least equally large problem in its own turn. Pastoral theology is problematic, in her view, if it is aimed primarily at producing scholars. The need is for insightful practitioners. She sees part of the merit of the programs of Clinical Pastoral Education that evolved from Boisen's work in the way in which they reveal that "the personal histories that people bring"[18] shape understandings of theology—a point about contextual theology.

Miller-McLemore's reassessment of Boisen's legacy also affirms that insight into an individual's problems can enable vision of wider social malaise. She cites Wayne Oates's comment that individuals may offer "a microscopic lab report" on social injustices. Pastoral theologies need to link up individual and social issues, and practitioners of a clerical paradigm might then find themselves well placed to act on what they learn, for churches have corporate means and position to initiate public transformation. The image of the web can highlight how both CPE and pastoral theology can bridge not only disciplines but what are sometimes regarded as separate audiences: the academy, the church, and society.

## Pastoral Theology and Public Theology

Miller-McLemore has also been among a number of writers in pastoral and practical theology who have explored the notion of "public theology," which is currently in vogue. Amongst different initiatives, a "Global Network of Public Theology"[19] has recently been established that connects academic institutions on several different continents, and that network has spawned a journal, *An International Journal of Public Theology*.[20] New courses and conferences on public theology are appearing within these and other theological institutions, and books on public theology are being published and promised. Indeed, "public theology" is a term with different genealogies in different settings, and hence has taken on a range of meanings. Another of its antecedents could be said to be the spirit of the encyclical *Gaudium et Spes*, promulgated by the Second Vatican Council of Roman Catholic bishops in the mid-1960s. The encyclical opens with the luminous affirmation that "the joys and the hopes, the griefs and the anxieties of the men of this age, especially those

---

18. Dykstra, *Images*, 8.
19. http://www.csu.edu.au/special/accc/about/gnpt/.
20. https://www.brill.nl/ijpt.

who are poor or in any way afflicted, these are the joys and hopes, the griefs and anxieties of the followers of Christ,"[21] and there is a sense in which public theology can be seen as a parallel development to Catholic social teaching. In any case, there are geographical as well as ecclesial nuances in public theology, such that its development in the USA is quite different from the ways in which it has emerged in Australia or the UK, for instance, with the former context one in which theoretical, "cognitive" understandings of the public sphere have been developed, and where a particular concern has been to resist the "privatization" of religion, whereas in the latter setting the emphasis has rather been on practical endeavors to engage umbrella cultures of which the churches are a part. In that latter context, it is firmly seen as a subbranch of practical theology. In both contexts, however, it can, allied to the liberationist tradition, be seen as a means of widening horizons beyond individuals.

### More Feminist Challenges

However, the descriptor "public" is deeply fraught with questions about the significance of gender. It can be used to suggest a somewhat undifferentiated realm, as if "public" is, as it were, a level playing field to which all have equal access and in which all have equal power. This is evidently not the case, as decades of feminist scholarship have insisted—and the reserve of some about the emerging genre of public theology is that it can sometimes appear to be quite willfully neglectful of such feminist insight.[22]

### Practical and Public Theology

It is significant, I think, that the idea of "public theology" is often organized as a substrand of "practical theology." Collections—like Duncan Forrester's *Truthful Action* and Elaine Graham's *Words Made*

---

21. Second Vatican Council, *Gaudium et spes* (The Pastoral Constitution on the Church in the Modern World), http://www.vatican.va/archive/hist_councils/ii_vatican_council /documents/vat-ii_const_19651207_gaudium-et-spes_en.html, accessed August 12, 2015
22. See Anita Monro and Stephen Burns, eds., *Public Theology and the Challenge of Feminism* (London: Routledge, 2014).

*Flesh*—include clusters of essays under the heading of "public theology." Notably, the same arrangement is found in a book by Stephen Pattison, his *Challenge of Practical Theology*. Returning to Pattison brings the chapter as it were full circle, and my next point underlines Bonnie Miller-McLemore's perception that public theology has developed differently in the UK and USA. I suspect that there is a characteristically British way of imagining the relationship between practical and public theologies, which Elaine Graham describes in terms of practical theology in the UK being permeated by a strong sense of what she, following Pattison, calls "the politics of pastoral care,"[23] as well as what she calls its "strongly 'public' tenor."[24] She elaborates: In Britain, practical theology has developed a distinctively multidisciplinary character "more richly embodied than in any other national context." It has resisted subdividing (into pastoral counseling, liturgy, and other streams sometimes included under the umbrella term "practical theology"); it has also flourished in the midst of widespread ecumenical theological education, and, "by virtue of establishment," in relation to a widely shared sense of the "permeability" of ministerial practice with strong emphasis on service in parishes as geographical areas, as opposed more narrowly to gathered congregations. Perhaps significantly for the approaches they champion, Forrester, Graham, and Pattison belong to established churches, and Forrester and Pattison are ordained ministers within their respective Church of Scotland and Church of England traditions.

For his part, Pattison, too, whose major work has been relating pastoral care and liberation theology, can readily be allied with the kind of liberationist public theology Forrester promotes, and like Graham, can be identified as often working closely with feminist perspectives. He is also acid about some constructs of public theology, so here is a taster. He critiques what he calls the ecclesial and academic confinement of theology—being either the "handmaid of ecclesiastical authority" or a "'monotechnic' environment." Together, he asserts, these conspire to

---

23. See Pattison, *Critique* and Pattison, *Liberation Theology*.
24. Elaine Graham, "Why Pastoral Theology Must Go Public," *Practical Theology* 1 (2008): 12.

theology's "poverty of listening" and reticence to learn: "prefer[ing]
to speak than to listen . . . theologians seem to have adopted the idea
that communicating is one-way—they should speak and others should
listen."[25] Moreover, the otiosity of this "perpetuates self-serving arro-
gance." Pattison is likely to have learned at least some of this from feminist and liberation theologies.

Public theology in these British expressions is more deeply indebted
to liberationist traditions than its versions elsewhere, perhaps. And in
Forrester especially, we also find a curious alliance with some emphases in the classical tradition, albeit Forrester's interest in worship does
not always seem to be fully integrated into assessments of his work.
Miller-McClemore's image of the living human web also links back
clearly, both critically and appreciatively, to the therapeutic tradition.
In different and related ways, both Forrester and Graham especially
understand public theology in terms of ministerial practice, and this may
be a particular alliance which is as yet waiting for more robust attention
in some contexts—Australia being an example, as there, discussion of
public theology has sometimes been more overtly concerned with "the
art of persuasion, of speaking into the social imagination and of winning
the right to be heard in a public marketplace of ideas."[26] The public
potential of pastoral ministry is an issue to which this book will turn in
a different way in part two. But first, a personal narrative, next, attempts
to gather reflections from across these first three chapters.

---

25. Stephen Pattison, "Public Theology: A Polemical Epilogue," in Stephen Pattison, *The
Challenge of Practical Theology: Collected Essays* (London: Jessica Kingsley, 2007), 212–28.
26. Clive Pearson, "The Public Comeback of God," in Ross Langmead, ed., *Reimagining
God and Mission: Perspectives from Australia* (Adelaide: ATF, 2007), 83–98. Note the
concentration of terms such as "conversation," "languages," "linguistics," word-centred
terms, in this essay, perhaps reflective of the ecclesiology from which this approach to
public theology is oriented. Note, too, the more doctrinal focus suggested for public
theology.

# Making the Connections:
# A Personal Reflection

As this survey of three different but related traditions of pastoral theology draws to a close, it will be clear that they have some quite distinctive emphases, as well as many points of overlap and interaction. All kinds of connections can be made between the different traditions, even as they mark out space from one another. To return to my optometrist analogy, my suggestion is that pastoral caregivers learn to think within each tradition in order then to be able to think between them, allowing criss-crosses, ziz-zags, and sloping from one to another to complement and question, to press or enlarge the value of one lens or another in particular circumstances.

At the same time, despite my opening vignettes, what the discussion of the traditions has not yielded is very much *immediate* reflection on action in *particular* pastoral situations. Our survey of traditions of pastoral theology has not been anything like a pastoral theology of particular actions in particular situations. It is worth noting, then, that akin to the kind of "agenda" of topics which marks systematic theology: God, Christ, Spirit, creation, redemption, church, sacraments, and so on, Carrie Doehring suggests that many if not most pastoral situations can in fact be categorized as concern with violence, loss, or compulsive forms of coping.[1] This is a helpful insight, in part because it resists an overly specific agenda, while at the same time suggesting that a certain kind of coherence can be found in many pastoral scenarios. The coherence is by no means an obvious comfort, however, given the potentially huge trauma involved in violence, loss, or compulsive forms of coping, and the distress manifest in any or all of them. At the same time, Doehring's loose typology does suggest that pastoral caregivers will oftentimes deal with a related, albeit broad, range of interhuman dynamics.

The traditions we have surveyed can be turned to these dynamics. In pastoral practice, the emphases of the different traditions can be used as lenses on various pastoral scenarios, so that any particular situation or issue—a specific instance of violence, loss, or a compulsive form of coping—is viewed from various angles: the angles of the therapeutic, classical, and liberationist traditions. In working out pastoral action in any such situation, regard might be given to the persons involved as living human documents, to their living human web, to the classical resources which the Christian tradition may yield to such persons, and to the enabling of engagement with their context so that they will not simply be adjusted to it, but liberated from or within it. That is, a fully rounded approach to the traditions is being commended, as a means by which pastoral practice can be habitually enriched and headlong actions, the implications of which are only partially thought through, can be forestalled by the mutually challenging insights of the traditions as these are brought into interaction with each other.

Yet more can be said about the three traditions. The therapeutic tradition, with its emphasis on reading the living human document, has an obvious focus on individual experience, even as that tradition has been reframed by an enlarged emphasis on the living human web. Yet even at its most individually oriented beginnings, it quickly developed an important emphasis which is a very significant legacy to later notions of public ministry. While the document upon which the therapeutic tradition focused was the patient, the tradition held an ambitious vision

---

1. Carrie Doehring, *The Practice of Pastoral Care: A Postmodern Approach* (Louisville, KY: Westminster John Knox Press, 2006).

of the pastor herself. She was to be a religious professional, with professional expertise to bring to a multidisciplinary diagnostic enterprise. While the individual patient was what the tradition focused upon, the pastor as the agent of change was being reconfigured as a professional with a role on the ward. She would be part of an interdisciplinary team, with a particular specialism to bring to the team. This is significant, for different reasons. First, the role of the minister is being situated not so much or only in the sanctuary—in the image of the second chapter, at the "altar"—she is set to work in intentional ways beyond the gathered congregation. The vision of ministry fostered by the Clinical Pastoral Education movement is a robust one, in which the minister is at home in nonecclesial settings, perhaps not ones which are fully public (psychiatric wards being in a certain way, almost cloistered, in order to shelter persons in their vulnerability), but certainly in ambiguous spaces, where religious language may not be the dominant or primary language, and where religious perspectives are expected to compete for interpretive power. In another sense, of course, by setting ministry intentionally and strategically among other professions, CPE can be thought of as revitalizing a public ministry. Secondly, Boisen was robust in his confidence that religious interpretation was needed of problems that presented with what might at first appear to be other manifestations. This is not perhaps "public theology" as this term would later come to be used, but it is unapologetic about the need for theological perspectives to be set in a wider context of exchange.

The classical tradition of course contests some of the marks of the therapeutic tradition, seeking to reassert that word and sacrament are the center of ministry. This is the tradition that tends to be most evidently represented in rites of ordination. In linking preaching, presidency, and pastoral care, Anglican theologies of "the ministry" tend to make classical alliances.

The liberationist tradition is most obviously public, even as constructs of "the public" might be critiqued from within the liberationist tradition as well as without. Whether or not notions of the public or public theology are invoked, the liberationist tradition underlines that pastoral care might involve sociopolitical action as well as sociopolitical analysis on the part of ministers. Yet even the classical tradition, which at first blush might seem least concerned with a wide orbit of ministry in which a gathered congregation is set, is also inscribed with a broader perspective. It should be remembered that Oden's own emphasis on classical expressions of pastoral care involves an albeit ancillary stress on the preciousness of diffuse Christian presence in happenchance circumstances of nonscheduled social interaction which is able to yield "serendipitous moments." Witness, service, and ministry to the broader community beyond the gathered congregation are clearly in Oden's sights, and his vision is replete with numerous examples. And the deepest memories of liturgical tradition, in Justin Martyr's witness, also impress the point that gathering involves various sendings from the gathering, and is concerned with the absent, the vulnerable, and the poor (see his 1 Apology 67). Even the classical tradition has impulses which orient ministry to the wider social world of any gathering around word and sacrament. The altar can be related to hospitals, roadwork, and many other settings.

What, then, if we took a pastoral scenario—or a cluster of them—and attempted such thinking, as some sort of illustration of what I have been commending? Many particular instances might serve as a focus, but so might a kind of composite that tries to connect individual encounters, such as might be encouraged by the wider perspectives at times strongly encouraged in the perspectives we have surveyed.

Much of my own adult life and ministry has been spent with people who are asylum seekers and refugees. The British government "settled" many refugees in the first parish in which I was an incumbent. In that parish, asylum seekers presented both at church and at the vicarage with many pressing needs for practical assistance, but also for advocacy, and sometimes for some sort of spiritual counsel. Among many examples, Iranian families already suffering from posttraumatic stress who then had bricks thrown through their windows by racist locals; Sri Lankan persons pleading for the church to make attempts to prevent their deportation; Congolese lamenting their lost loved ones whose whereabouts had been unknown since they scrambled to escape violent rampages through their villages. There were many stressful and distressing narratives and encounters, and Doehring's categories of violence, loss, and coping were all present at once in too many cases. And there were some happier happenings. For example, when I myself started to visit asylum seekers in the parish, I had a regular meeting with a group of Afghan men in which we drank their strong coffee and talked about scriptures, theirs and mine; celebrations in which the church gave its space to asylum seekers wanting to cook a meal (in fact, a feast) in thanksgiving for local people's care—an occasion in which the needy turned provider, the helped ones turned givers; and the numerous asylum seekers who became members of the local church, bringing their dialects, testimonies, and traditions to reshape our common life in Christ. Many, indeed, had long been Christians, and some had fled contexts in which Christians were persecuted, though others suffered persecution for their sexual orientation, or ethnicity, among other reasons.

When asylum seekers started to arrive in the parish, I, with others in the local congregation, sought the advice and example of other parishes dealing with similar influx of need. We went to visit welcoming programs, groups teaching English as a second language, and simple English language church services, all aimed at supporting new populations of asylum seekers, and all efforts that we would ourselves explore. Richer churches in the diocese were called upon not least for their charitable giving, but also for the time of their volunteers, and the expertise of lay members in social work and law, child care and translation, and much else. What we have called above the therapeutic tradition of pastoral care was crucial to hearing the stories, sometimes ghastly and awful, often of great faith and tenacity, that asylum seekers conveyed. Having their stories heard was, for some if not for many, part of finding dignity in life after and in what continued to be very taxing circumstances. The "living human documents" of their experience—full of narratives that kept alive convictions and traditions, as well as oftentimes plenty of questions and confusion, and much else—were crucial. The fragility of life that the stories sometimes told, of immense and harrowing loss and grief and pain, could call forth reverence. In light of some of the stories, it might well be expected that amongst all the many needs for adjustment to new life, inherited theological convictions were among those things that came to be adjusted.[2] And sometimes, of course, the "living human web" of refugees had been completely and even brutally shattered, and yet, sometimes, stories of scripture and of shared Christian faith could be profoundly sustaining, and also the basis for the new fusion of bonds with strangers from very different parts of the globe whose experience had been altogether different. Indeed, church sometimes became a vital part of finding or making a new living human web of connection.

In these scenarios I am beginning to describe, the classical tradition of pastoral care was at play in these experiences of church. The stories of the Bible, the ritual of communion—albeit perhaps culturally different—were sometimes a major part of "home" that could in one form or another be found in a new place, maybe even helping that new place to become home. Recognizing that many of the asylum seekers were Christian people and starting a simple prayer group became significant parts of parish life. As people from all over the world gathered for a simple meal and sometimes halting conversation, regular Christian practices were frequently deeply moving, as people prayed in the language most familiar to them, the many different mother tongues not always understood by others, but infused with emotion that communicated nonetheless. And the joining of voices speaking many different languages in the Lord's Prayer could be beautiful in its glossalaic way, as brief pauses for breath between lines seemed to hold the prayer together despite the many different sounds. Quite apart from the beauty of this, aspects of the classical tradition were present in other ways, not least in the pressing demands upon the church for what Herbert might call a "complete" ministry—not just essentials such as time and space for

---

2. Susanna Snyder, *Asylum Seeking, Migration and Church* (Farnham: Ashgate, 2012) is the major work to engage asylum seekers from theological perspective. My own slight *Welcoming Asylum Seekers* (Cambridge: Grove, 2004) relates some of my own adjustment. In North American contexts, Mark Adams, et al., *Bishops at the Border: Pastoral Responses to Immigration* (New York: Seabury, 2013) includes much disturbing and also profoundly moving material about Christian engagement with immigrants.

prayer, but for enactment of belief and spirituality in practical provisions of different kinds, and of advocacy.

Advocacy, with landlords, schools, medical providers, council authorities, and local services, and not least sometimes accompaniment and support at appeals hearings, were all expressions of what was termed above the liberationist tradition. Herbert's language of complete ministry already presses in this direction, but writers such as Miller-McLemore and especially Pattison help us to appreciate what might be involved in its contemporary manifestations. Sociopolitical aspects of care, including change for the betterment of what Miller-McLemore coins the living human web in which persons live, all unfolded from the kinds of encounter asylum seekers and refugees sought with the local church. In Forrester's understanding of public theology, the testimony of the poor, spoken in their terms and using their own idioms, is crucially important, and it represents a kind of advance on Boisen's understanding of the living human document. Whereas he considers the "document" of personal experience in the context of the pastoral relationship and beyond that the workings of the hospital care team, Forrester places that document in the guardianship of the church, goading the church to carry the narratives of the living human document into public discourse, enabling the voices of persons of less powerful voice to be amplified, ensuring that they are heard. Making space for such testimony and then pressing for it to be heard amongst wider circles of the public was one "service of the poor" that the church was able to perform in relationship to asylum seekers and refugees, doing so at local level but also in consort with others regionally. By wading into public debate to carry the perspectives of the poor on political decisions, social provisions, welfare structures, and public truculence to share resources, the church can contribute at wider levels too, including pressing for change in policy that affirms dignity and places care at points of need.

To return my opening vignette: It would be hard to convey easily to Earl in the car showroom how a rector might be involved in many various ways with therapeutic, classical, and liberationist traditions of pastoral care. But hopefully what a seeming stranger to Christian communities like Earl becomes able to see in the church's public ministers would be the concern for human dignity and healing, means of grace, and social justice that these traditions at their best represent. How that will be so is not always straightforward, but the need for public transformation of pastors' roles is acute, as the incident on the train in the other vignette from my introduction suggests. As we proceed, part two considers further sensitivity to some of the symbols in which public ministry swirls.

# PART TWO

# PUBLIC MINISTRY

## Always Oneself,
## Never Only Oneself

"To care" has a double meaning, involving both anxieties and love. "To carry cares" is a now somewhat old-fashioned, quaint manner of speaking that captures something of the link between care and anxiety. Care is, as it were, heavy, burdensome, troubling. This idiom of care remains lively for some persons in their continued recollection of biblical and traditional injunctions to "cast cares" upon God.

"To care for" suggests the other side of care, its link with love and affection. Though this manner of speaking may refer to the relatively mundane, even flighty and fanciful, at least sometimes "to care for" another person, or an object, or an activity, may suggest deep attraction, preference, choice, enfolding the deepest of human desires and delight.

So our language enables us to think in different ways of "care." Caring relationships are marked by both anxiety and love. Such relationships may be profoundly draining, depleting, and worrisome for persons who offer care. Caring relationships may also bear witness to extraordinary commitment, faithfulness, and joy. In many such relationships, anxiety and love, depletion and joy, faithfulness and exhaustion may be deeply entangled.

Pastoral relationships entail additional entanglements, in that they are overlain with symbolic associations funded by the very word "pastoral," which has to do with the work of keeping sheep. These associations are the focus of the next chapter. These symbolic associations remain a rich resource for pastoral care, if only for the caregiver herself—if perhaps not always for the ones for whom she cares. Pastoral care offered by Christian persons engaged with the symbolic associations of "shepherding" may well, of course, be in hospitals or at work, in prisons or football clubs or shopping malls, and the caregivers themselves—by virtue of their own engagement with the Christian tradition—will be concerned with the shepherding associations of their work in such settings. Others too—even in urban centers distant from agricultural practices—may also be engaged with ideas of shepherding, inherited from the Christian tradition, because they are regularly recalled in scripture and public worship which both strongly mediate associations with imagery of shepherding. So a Christian pastoral caregiver finds herself in a swirl of images, in which she is herself engaged, and in which others may also be engaged. Moreover, a pastoral caregiver not only finds herself among symbols, *she is herself a symbol.* In her work of pastoral care, a Christian caregiver is never simply "herself," but entangled with what the tradition makes of her. She is what Gordon Lathrop defines as "a gathering place for communal encounter with wider meaning."[1] At least, a pastoral caregiver *intends* to be such a symbol, so that her care may enable anxiety to be shared, cast off, eased, and love be enacted, witnessed, manifest. At the same time, she remains always herself, even as she is not only herself.[2] Various personal dimensions of the pastoral caregiver's experience

---

1. Gordon W. Lathrop, *The Pastor: A Spirituality* (Minneapolis, MN: Fortress Press, 2006), 5.
2. For more, see Stephen Burns, "Yearning Without Saying a Word: Unembarrassed Presiding in Liturgy," *Worship* 85 (2011): 1–16.

are the focus of the final chapter. And so part two contemplates "the pastor as symbol" and the "the person as pastor." In various ways, the following chapters contemplate aspects of the classical tradition of pastoral care, explore aspects of the "living human document" of the caregiver herself, and consider the impact of the sociopolitical contexts in which she offers care.

# CHAPTER 4

# The Pastor as Symbol

The priest picks his way
Through the parish. Eyes watch him
From windows, from the farms;
Hearts wanting him to come near.
The flesh rejects him.

Women, pouring from the black kettle,
Stir up the whirling-grounds
Of their thoughts; offer him a dark
Filling in their smiling sandwich.

Priests have a long way to go.
The people wait for them to come
To them over the broken glass
Of their vows, making them pay
With their sweat's coinage for their correction.

He goes up a green lane
Through growing birches; lambs cushion
His vision. He comes slowly down
In the dark, feeling the cross warp
In his hands; hanging on it his thought's icicles.

'Crippled soul', do you say? looking at him
From the mind's height; limping through life
On his prayers. "There are other people
In the world, sitting at table
Contented, though the broken body
And the shed blood are not the menu."

"Let it be so," I say. "Amen and amen."[1]

R. S. Thomas (1913–2000) was one of the most highly acclaimed religious poets of the late twentieth century, beginning his publishing career when priest in the Welsh valleys. He continued to write poetry while a long after his retirement as a clergyperson in 1978. Numerous of his poems reflect on his work as a priest, including this one from his 1968 collection, *Not That He Brought Flowers*. In "The Priest," Thomas paints a bleak image of his subject: The minister is observed, both beckoned and spurned; he evokes some depth—the "darkness behind the smile"—but it is an ambiguous depth. The cross, the holy communion, and pastoral scenes—"lambs cushion his vision"—shape his own symbolic landscape. He has a coldness, and a darkness, about him: His strangeness is not warm and bright. Any brightness in the poem seems to belong to "contented" others, while the priest himself seems to make do with the paucity of a eucharistic menu.

Interestingly, it is the very bleakness of Thomas's vision that has recently been powerfully evoked in David Sylvian's strange and interesting recording "Manafon." Minimal, sparse jazz improvisations underscore lyrical images of Thomas's life, sung in plaintive tones, all faithful to Thomas's texts. As if echoing those in "The Priest" who see their minister coming, now "farmer's wives . . . tell the kids to lower their voices, and pretend that they are out." And in Sylvian's depiction, Thomas's own wife "was a painter, but now she stains the altar black,"[2] providing her own dark surrounds for the priest's bleakness.

---

1. R. S. Thomas, *Selected Poems* (London: Granada, 1979), 119; quoted in Stephen Pattison, *A Critique of Pastoral Care* (London: SCM Press, 1993), 152.
2. http://www.davidsylvian.com/texts/lyrics_and_poetry/manafon_lyrics.html.

Notwithstanding the dourness of Thomas's imagery, the poem has numerous resonances with the twenty-third psalm, which in the Coverdale translation of the 1662 Book of Common Prayer reads: "THE Lord is my shepherd : therefore can I lack nothing. . ."[3]

The lambs "cushion[ing his] vision" perhaps remind Thomas's priest of the gentle presence of the divine, an accompanying shepherd according to the psalm. Even so, many of the resonances between the psalm and the poem are harsher, even seeming sometimes to be inversions. So the psalm's green pastures are echoed in "The Priest"'s farm, and the green lane, but the psalm's still waters become the poem's grounds whirling in black tea. And the rod and staff of the psalm are transposed in the poem into a different kind of correction, not now guiding to comfort but overseeing work that must pay.

In fact, the theme of correction runs through a number of Thomas's poems, so that another concerned with ministry—"The Country Clergy"—depicts God making good the forgetfulness of parishioners, whose priests "left no books" as a "memorial to their lonely thought in grey parishes," but instead wrote on hearts and minds "sublime words too soon forgotten." Thomas's poem on the country clergy ends that "God in his time or out of time will correct" the legacy of the ministers' memorial. Quite apart from anything else, Thomas's images of ministers leaving no books and writing on hearts offer a complement to the notion of the living human document we have encountered in earlier pages of this book.

Perhaps until the making good that Thomas speaks of takes place, however, Psalm 23's laden table prepared by the Lord is experienced, at least by the priest, as sparse, for it seems that it is others—the contented—whose cups run over. Psalm 23's closing note of praise—"thy loving-kindness and mercy shall follow me all the days of my life"—are, to put it mildly, much more muted in the poem, shrunk down to a resigned amen. The priest's following is not abundant, but injured, "limping," reminiscent

---

3. The BCP 1662 translation of the psalm is easily accessible at: https://churchofengland .org/prayer-worship/worship/book-of-common-prayer/the-psalter/psalms-22-23.aspx.

of the book of Genesis's story of the divine adversary with whom Jacob wrestles, and by whom he is bruised (Genesis 32:22–32).

## Broken Symbols

In his poetry, Thomas movingly depicts something of the ambiguities and difficulties of pastoral work. At the very least, he reminds his readers that "traditional" pastoral caregivers can cut very strange figures. It is this recognition of strangeness, and a wider sense of alienation, which perhaps has led to some attempts in some traditions to do away with some of the long-standing symbolic associations of the clergy.

Contemporary struggles to identify a role for ordained ministers have sometimes involved a ditching of traditional symbols—clerical and liturgical vesture and what Martyn Percy has called clerical "plumage,"[4] for instance—and may be done in the interests of "inculturation," or in order to present as "nearer" to other people, less remote, less strange, perhaps. Part of this impulse might come from recognition that clergypersons have, no less than others, misused their power, and twist symbols intended to evoke trust, to abuse the trust and bodies of the vulnerable young. If such contemporary clergy think of themselves as "set apart" in some ways, it is, at least in some places,[5] not in terms of attire. Yet clergy who ditch the use of "plumage" like clerical collars may not be averse to making their presence known in other ways. An entirely inculturated ministry, which simply reflects rather than challenges the problems of the larger culture, can hardly be worth having, and in with respect to that conviction, the "strangeness" of plumage may yet have a part to play in signaling resistance.[6]

---

4. Martyn Percy, *Clergy: Origins of the Species* (London: Continuum, 2006), 89–92.
5. For reflection on one such context, see Stephen Burns, "Formation for Ordained Ministry: Out of Touch?" in *Indigenous Australia and the Unfinished Business of Theology*, ed. Jione Havea (New York: Palgrave, 2014), 151–66 and also Stephen Burns, "Ministry," in *An Informed Faith*, ed. William W. Emilsen (Melbourne: Mosaic Press, 2014), 37–68.
6. See http://www.elca.org/Growing-In-Faith/Worship/Learning-Center/LWF-Nairobi-Statement.aspx.

Whatever, the particular symbol of the clerical collar is itself a fairly recent innovation, often ascribed to a nineteenth-century Church of Scotland minister, Donald MacLeod, although with an older variant dating back to the seventeenth century, with that earlier version made popular by Anglo-Catholic clergy of the Church of England. And if some contemporary clergy have wished to disassociate themselves from this legacy, and so have adopted a more incognito approach to their presence in their local communities, it remains, as Robert Gribben suggests, that

> few people decide [what symbolic dress they may wear] by reason and logic: like all symbols, dress affects us at a level deeper than the intellect. It is also the writer's view that until people know what is involved is such decision, they are bound by what is familiar—and that may be very limiting and partial. Only when we know what we are doing are we free to do it.[7]

It also remains that their status as clergy, the "set apartness" to which ordination calls them, must be enacted, one way or another, if they are to be effective in their roles.[8] The point made by a sociological study of English Anglican clergy in the late 1970s stands true in another time and place: For while it may not be, as that study suggests, that as "a public person [a clergyperson] alone in our society, wears a distinctive uniform at all times," it *is* the case that "when he (sic) discards the uniform, as many clergymen do today, he evades the problem posed by his marginality, but he does not solve it."[9]

Whether clergy associate themselves with symbols such as the collar, or not, as pastoral caregivers, they are, as Gordon Lathrop insists, to some extent always a symbol.[10] They are, in Lathrop's terms, "a

---

7. http://assembly.uca.org.au/worship/resources/guidelines-for-worship/28-liturgicaldress.html.

8. The notable Uniting Church in Australia liturgical theologian Robert W. Gribben provides a robust discussion of liturgical and clerical dress in his paper for the Uniting Church Commission on Liturgy (as it was then named), at http://assembly.uca.org.au/worship/resources/guidelines-for-worship/28-liturgicaldress.html.

9. Quoted by Percy, *Clergy*, 29.

10. Gordon W. Lathrop, *The Pastor: A Spirituality* (Minneapolis, MN: Fortress Press, 2006), 5.

gathering place for communal encounter with wider meaning."[11] Part of the larger association they carry is of course the abuse in which some clergy have engaged. A clerical collar might make these and other problematic associations more upfront than other kinds of casual attire, but any Christian minister, whatever she wears, must be ready to engage other persons with the ambivalence of the history and company they represent. Yet a more positive side to the wider meaning that pastoral caregivers, ordained or not, carry with them is the hopeful resourcefulness of the wider Christian tradition. Simply put, pastors are never independent, never alone in their work, for what the book of Hebrews calls "a great cloud of witnesses" (Hebrews 12.1) gathered around Christ and infused by the Spirit is part of that to which they give verbal or nonverbal testimony. Even so, not so "great" herself, a pastor is aware that, while always a symbol, she is, as Lathrop has it, albeit a broken symbol, seeking to be but never entirely "transparent" to the central things of word and sacrament "for which she or he was appointed in the first place."[12] As such, a minister of pastoral care—lay or ordained—is, to borrow a phrase from Gail Ramshaw's writings, always "mythically more" than herself.[13]

## Shepherding in Scripture and Liturgy

The word "pastoral" comes from images of shepherding. In the New Testament, pastors are referred to as shepherds (Ephesians 4:11), and this biblical correlation between shepherding and pastoring has been embedded in liturgy, and particularly in ordination rites, since early times. But the liturgy's, like scripture's, language of shepherding is not simply related to interhuman relationships. One memorable opening prayer from the Roman Catholic tradition gathers a number of the foci in the biblical range of images of shepherds, addressing God who "in

---

11. Lathrop, *Pastor*, 5.
12. Lathrop, *Pastor*, 6.
13. Gail Ramshaw, "Pried Open by Prayer," in *Liturgy and the Moral Self: Humanity at Full Stretch before God: Essays in Honor of Don E. Saliers*, ed. E. Byron Anderson and Bruce T. Morrill (Collegeville, MN: Liturgical Press, 1998), 174.

Christ [has] sought us with a shepherd's heart" and in whom the prayers "rejoice . . . to be found and restored. . ."[14]

God and Christ are also "shepherds."

## Scripture

The range of biblical images of shepherding is, of course, much wider than in reference to Christian leaders. It is also used of the divine. The one whom the twenty-third psalm praises is shepherd. God is the shepherd of Israel. And Ezekiel 34 relates a prophecy in which Ezekiel is commanded to speak against "the shepherds of Israel," who have been "feeding [themselves]" rather than their flocks:

> You eat the fat, you clothe yourselves with the wool, you slaughter the fatlings; but you do not feed the sheep. You have not strengthened the weak, you have not healed the sick, you have not bound up the injured, you have not brought back the strayed, you have not sought the lost, but with force and harshness you have ruled them (Ezekiel 34:3–4).

Consequently, Ezekiel declares that God is "against the shepherds" and will, Godself, be a shepherd to the people:

> For thus says the Lord GOD: I myself will search for my sheep, and will seek them out. As shepherds seek out their flocks when they are among their scattered sheep, so I will seek out my sheep. I will rescue them from all the places to which they have been scattered on a day of clouds and thick darkness. I will bring them out from the peoples and gather them from the countries, and will bring them into their own land; and I will feed them on the mountains of Israel, by the watercourses, and in all the inhabited parts of the land. I will feed them with good pasture, and the mountain heights of Israel shall be their pasture; there they shall lie down in good grazing land, and they shall feed on rich pasture on the mountains of Israel. I myself will be the shepherd of my sheep, and I will make them lie down, says the Lord GOD. I will seek

14. International Commission on English in the Liturgy, *Opening Prayers: Scripture-related Collects for Lectionary Cycles A, B and C* (Norwich: Canterbury Press, 1997), 57.

the lost, and I will bring back the strayed, and I will bind up the injured, and I will strengthen the weak, but the fat and the strong I will destroy. I will feed them with justice (Ezekiel 34:11–16).

Moreover, it is not that, once the bad shepherds have been ditched, the people will simply have an unmediated relationship with God. According to the prophecy, David will mediate between God and the people as a trustworthy shepherd, indeed royal "prince" (Ezekiel 34:24).

All of this shapes the wider context in which correlations between shepherds and persons in pastoral roles need to be remembered. Psalm 23 is perhaps the best known portion of scripture, and part of the imagination of many persons who do not regularly participate in church activities. It continues to shape public imagination, because—not least in funeral rites—it is presented at an interface between the Judeo-Christian tradition's depictions of the divine and opportunities of ministry among persons far beyond those who worship regularly in Christian communities. Such people may not worship very often, and may perhaps turn to the church's representatives only at times of personal crisis, grief, or need, but they may yet carry something of the church's memory that "the LORD is my shepherd."

Such persons may at times be open to accept accompaniment, encouragement, and guidance from representative ministers of the church, even as such ministers, lay or ordained, might not be imagined as "shepherds." Yet within the context of depicting the divine as a shepherd, the Bible does portray certain kinds of leaders as shepherds. This is a multitextured scriptural theme, with roots in the agricultural context of biblical cultures, Hebrew call stories of shepherds—like David—become sovereigns to their people, and the ways such narratives are layered into testimony as to the meaning of Jesus. In the first place, the wider cultural context that shapes biblical ideas of shepherding can be seen in so far as the Bible is not the only ancient writing to associate leadership with shepherding. As one other well-known example, Plato's *Republic* makes the same correlation.[15]

---

15. Gail Ramshaw, *Treasures Old and New: Images in the Lectionary* (Minneapolis, MN: Fortress Press, 2002), 366.

In fact, the Hebrew Bible engages in "stereotypical Near Eastern figurative speech" about shepherds.[16] Second, as Gail Ramshaw points out, the connection between shepherding and kingship is fused in particular biblical characters such as David, and also extends to the possibility that imagery of a royal scepter evolved from that of the shepherd's crook. Shepherding care and monarchical rulership were intertwined. Third, this background focuses on Gospel memories of Jesus, which gather and reframe the Hebrew inheritance. In the synoptic Gospels, Jesus is stirred by recognition that the people are "like sheep without a shepherd" (Matthew 9:36), and he meets their needs, as a shepherd would. Tales of shepherding are part of Jesus's own teaching and preaching—so lost sheep are found (Luke 15:3–7), and (in his "royal" parable) sheep and goats are separated (Matthew 25:31–46). In Johannine testimony, Jesus not only proclaims himself as shepherd (John 10:11), but contrasts his goodness with the counterfeit care of "thieves and bandits" and "hired hands"—thereby both being aligned with the character of the divine and being distanced from the like of the false shepherds who provoke the prophecy of Ezekiel 34. According to John, the goodness of Jesus as shepherd is confirmed in terms of his willingness to "lay down his life for the sheep" (John 10:11). Later in John's Gospel, there is an explicit link between shepherding and leadership, as the risen Jesus emphatically commands Peter to "feed [his] lambs/sheep" (John 21:15–17), as the disciple is commanded to a mediatorial role akin to the one assigned to David in Ezekiel.

Beyond the evangelists' writings, what is presented as the core of New Testament *kerygma* casts Jesus not so much as shepherd but as a sheep, indeed a lamb to the slaughter. So Lucan memory of the Acts of the Apostles has them announcing their message with direct reference to Isaian traditions of the suffering servant, as one who gives himself to suffering with silent dignity, "like a sheep before its shearers" (Isaiah 53:7 and Acts 8:32). The link in Acts and John that relates shepherding imagery to death later pulled in at least two directions. On the one hand,

---

16. Ramshaw, *Treasures*, 366.

shepherds feature in early Christian tales of those who, like Jesus, give their lives. So Perpetua, at her martyrdom, saw

> a gray-haired man . . . in shepherd's garb; tall he was, and milk-ing sheep. And standing around him were many thousands of people clad in white garments. He raised his head, looked at me, and said: "I am glad you have come, my child." He called me over to him and gave me, as it were, a mouthful of the milk he was drawing, and I took it into my cupped hands and consumed it. And all those who stood around said "Amen!" At the sound of this word I came to, with the taste of something sweet still in my mouth. I told this to my brother, and we realized that we would have to suffer, and that from now on we would no longer have any hope in this life.[17]

Such narratives relate that in the early Christian imagination God was believed to remain as a shepherd to the faithful ones. On the other hand, the idea of Jesus as good shepherd was amplified in so far as it inspired the earliest art of young Christian communities. Images of Christ as good shepherd certainly predate the centrality of the cross as the most widely used Christian symbol, perhaps because with relative close-ness to the execution of Jesus, the instrument of his murder was simply regarded as being too grisly to be redeemed in pictures. Evidently, early catacomb depictions of Jesus were modeled on David, who is described in a book of Samuel as handsome and ruddy (1 Samuel 16:12). The Greek word for "good" also means "beautiful," and early depictions of Christ as good shepherd present him as youthful and vigorous, as in the well-known extant image from the Catacomb of San Callisto, Rome.

### Liturgy

If the environment of worship—the catacombs—featured shepherding images, so did other dimensions of worship. Ordination is the most obvi-ous example, in which associations between pastors (by whatever name) and shepherds over time became evermore deeply embedded. The Book

---

17. Ramshaw, *Treasures*, 365.

of Common Prayer of 1662, which has borne enormous influence on English speaking worshippers across the world, uses portions of Matthew 9 and John 10 as its scripture reading at the ordination of priests, and immediately follows the reading with a charge to the ordained that

> the holy Lessons taken out of the Gospel, and the writings of the Apostles, [teach] of what dignity, and of how great importance this Office is, whereunto ye are called. And now again we exhort you, in the Name of our Lord Jesus Christ, that ye have in remembrance, into how high a Dignity, and to how weighty an Office and Charge ye are called: that is to say, to be Messengers, Watchmen, and Stewards of the Lord; to teach, and to premonish, to feed and provide for the Lord's family; to seek for Christ's sheep that are dispersed abroad, and for his children who are in the midst of this naughty world, that they may be saved through Christ for ever. Have always therefore printed in your remembrance, how great a treasure is committed to your charge. For they are the sheep of Christ, which he bought with his death, and for whom he shed his blood.[18]

## Ordination Rites

The alliance between shepherding and presbyteral (priestly) ministry continues into contemporary ordination rites. Before considering the ordination rites of The Episcopal Church, and to provide more context for that focus, we might first take in some ecumenical perspectives.

The ordination of "presbyters, usually called ministers" in the British Methodist Church praises God for "shepherding" God's people and charges ministers to "be shepherds to the flock of Christ" before almost immediately asserting that Christ himself is "Chief Shepherd."[19]

---

18. The Book of Common Prayer 1662, the rights in which are vested in the Crown. Reproduced by permission of the Crown's Patentee, Cambridge University Press. Please see: https://www.churchofengland.org/prayer-worship/worship/book-of-common-prayer /the-form-and-manner-of-making,-ordaining-and-consecrating-of-bishops,-priests-and -deacons/the-ordering-of-priests.aspx. Accessed August 12, 2015.
19. Methodist Church of Great Britain, *Methodist Worship Book* (Peterborough: Methodist Publishing House, 1999), 305, 308, 308.

Eucharistic prayer on the occasion of the ordination in turn names
Christ as "true Shepherd."[20] In the Uniting Church in Australia's service
for the ordination of Ministers of the Word (which corresponds to the
order widely designated ecumenically as presbyter[21]) the ordained are
charged that "taking Christ the Good Shepherd as your example, you
are called to lead God's people in worship, witness and service; to equip
them for their ministry and mission; and to work with them in building up the body of Christ."[22] In the Uniting Church services, scripture
portions include a number that focus on shepherding imagery, including
Psalm 23, and portions of Ezekiel 34 and John 10. Once more, then, the
imagery of shepherding is overlaid on the work of presbyteral ministry.
This is characteristic of the ways in which shepherding imagery comes
to be concentrated form in relation to expressions of Christian ministry. It may be present in association with various pastoral roles, but it
tends to be distilled in most concentrated form in relation to presbyteral
(priestly) ministry.

The British Methodist ordination service for deacons accents themes
of servanthood instead of shepherding images. Indeed, it is devoid of references to shepherding. Likewise, the Methodist services of admission of
lay preachers, which follow the ordination services as the book unfolds,
contains no shepherding imagery. Such imagery reemerges in the book's
next rite, the annual commissioning of pastoral visitors and class leaders,
in which God is praised for the gift of Christ as "Shepherd and Savior,"[23]
but in which the imagery of shepherd is *not* directly overlaid, as in presbyteral ordination, upon human persons. Within the terms of the service itself, "pastoral care" is correlated with "comfort and support,"[24] a
rather more restrained association than the sense of shepherding that is
applied to the pastoral visitors' and class leaders' ordained counterparts.

---

20. *Methodist Worship Book*, 309.
21. See http://www.anglican.org.au/Web/Website.nsf/files/Anglican-Uniting%20Dialogue%20-%20'For%20the%20Sake%20of%20the%20Gospel'/$FILE/Report%20to%20Standing%20Committee%20on%20For%20the%20Sake%20of%20the%20Gospel.pdf.
22. http://assembly.uca.org.au/worship/resources/order-service-in-church.html.
23. *Methodist Worship Book*, 346
24. *Methodist Worship Book*, 345.

Nevertheless, there is an element of priesthood about this ministry too, in so far as it is related, "as are all Christians" (as *Baptism, Eucharist, and Ministry* says), ordained and lay alike, both to the priesthood of Christ and the priesthood of the Church.

What we see in these examples is a concentrating of shepherding responsibilities with those ordained presbyters, and an intensification of the symbolic freight that priests are asked to carry. Perhaps no ordination rite has done this more so, though, than that of the Anglican Church in Aotearoa New Zealand and Polynesia. While selected scripture readings for the ordination sometimes—not always—use shepherding imagery, the texts for prayer speak rather of those "called to be pastors."[25] But what the service calls "The Commitment" culminates in an astonishing charge:

> Follow Christ whose servant you are. Share the burden of those whose cross is heavy. You are marked as a person who proclaims that among the truly blessed are the poor, the troubled, the powerless, the persecuted. You must be prepared to be what you proclaim.[26]

This startling descriptor calls a priest to be congruent with Jesus's Beatitudes, and its image of cross-carrying relates to Jesus's own talk of laying down his life for "his sheep." Agrarian, arguably outmoded, language has been avoided in the New Zealand rite, but for those who know their scriptures, the demands of pastoral ministry are amplified rather than diluted.

### Funeral Rites

In continuity with Perpetua meeting the shepherd at her death, as well as the shepherd scrawled on to catacomb walls, the language of shepherding also came to be continually revivified in funeral rites. This provides another liturgical focus to set alongside the imagery of shepherding in relation to (presbyteral) ordination, and means that whether or not ministers who lead funerals are themselves presbyters, all are,

---

25. *A New Zealand Prayer Book* (Auckland: Collins, 1989), 901.
26. *New Zealand Prayer Book*, 907.

by virtue of their role in funeral rites, placed in a symbolic melee in which shepherding imagery continues to be present, through use of the twenty-third psalm, perhaps, and in other ways. So in continuity with the tradition liturgies around the event of death strongly assert the continuing faithful shepherding presence of God. For example, in the Church of England's *Common Worship* range includes various prayers of commendation, including one for use with a dying person, in which Christ is asked to acknowledge "a sheep of [his] own fold," "a lamb of [his] own flock," and to enfold the dying one in his arms of mercy.[26]

Rites in some other churches reflect a certain hesitancy about overlaying the language of sheep and lambs onto adults (which most people are at the time of their death). There may well be understandable reserve about any possible patronizing tone.

### Eucharistic Rites

For some persons, too, the context of Christian worship also keeps another range of shepherding imagery in play. Committed members of congregational life encounter in the Eucharist a sense of Jesus not only as shepherd but as "lamb of God"—another Johannine descriptor. The *Agnus Dei* in the communion rite's action of fraction makes this association. Some invitations to communion not only echo but intensify the *Agnus Dei*: The Roman rite has the priest announce as he holds the host toward the people, "Behold the Lamb of God, behold him who takes away the sins of the world," and the Presbyterian-founded Iona Community, on the western coast of Scotland, somewhat surprisingly departs from a typical Protestant hesitation expressed in a reframing of this gesture with the words which make a less "localized" affirmation, like "Jesus is the Lamb of God who takes away the sins of the world"[27] with a text more akin to the Roman sensibility: "Look, look, here is your Lord coming to you in bread and wine."[28] Yet however traditions tinker

---

27. Anglican Church of Australia, *A Prayer Book for Australia* (Alexandria: Broughton Books, 1995), 146.
28. Iona Community, *A Wee Worship Book* (Glasgow: Wild Goose Publications, [3] 1989).

with the wording of the Roman rite, they all invoke a certain kind of shepherding imagery at a point of breaking—tearing or snapping bread, a symbol of vulnerability—which makes its own contribution to how pastoral symbols range across liturgical celebration.

## Scripture and Liturgy Interacting

What we can see in these examples is that liturgies juxtapose a range of images of shepherding, just as does scripture. This is true of scripture as what we may now recognize as a whole but also of particular instances, such as Revelation 7:17, in which the divine figure in the vision is both shepherd and lamb: "The Lamb at the center of the throne will be their shepherd." And this shepherding-lamb figure is in the same verse depicted as enacting pastoral and sacramental actions: wiping eyes dry of tears, and leading others to the waters of life. So the liturgical repertoire turns the scriptural images, and keeps what are already fluid images shifting once again.

This unsettled background to the use of shepherding imagery in scripture and liturgy is important in that, as Gail Ramshaw suggests, "we do well to monitor our use of the adjective pastoral and the adverb pastorally, which come sometimes to mean little more than nice."[29] That is, liturgy and scripture resist any simple sentimentalization of the descriptor "pastoral," and the shifting context in which liturgy turns a range of biblical imagery (just as the compilation of the scriptures enfolded a range of shepherding images already at use in liturgy) and can animate a pastor's understanding of her role. Breaking and death are obvious key words that reveal that not all of what is suggested about pastoral themes in liturgical and biblical tradition is easy, or "nice."

While noting the appeal and enigma of biblical pastoral imagery, one interesting instance remains to be mentioned. It relates in particular to the Lucan parable of the lost sheep, which depicts Jesus carrying a sheep back to the fold—itself a popular focus of stained glass and other

---

29. Ramshaw, *Treasures*, 368.

art forms. In a discussion that has taken place in various online locations, it has commonly been suggested that this action, in its context in Jesus's time and place, would have involved the shepherd breaking the sheep's legs in order to foster its dependency.[30] The shepherd carrying the sheep is no simple "gentle" figure, but one who causes pain, albeit for the long-term security of his dependent. Whatever truth is in this tradition, it points to some quite unsentimental associations of shepherding—and, whatever it might mean for the safety of sheep, in dynamics of transference to human persons needs to be questioned because of its inherent violence. The brutality of the image may of course in part be corrected by use of other images, kept in play alongside others, kept in check by those others as they are kept shifting, in the liturgy, and not least the lectionary. But the violence of this image and its inappropriateness if singled out as a pastoral image to shape "care," is itself enough to invoke a constant need, as Gail Ramshaw says, for "more layers, more shading, more connotations, to the shepherd, the flock and the lamb,"[31] such as this chapter has suggested.

## Public Representation

Given the symbolic associations of shepherding, a Christian pastoral caregiver is always representing something more than her or his own personal anxiety or love. She or he may be called, commissioned, and charged to represent the Church, and this may involve either an explicit or implicit appointment, in certain scenarios, to accept the awesome responsibility to represent the divine. This notion is an uncomfortable one for many persons who find themselves called to pastoral care, and that they struggle with such associations is a good thing, as any easy appropriation of a notion like "representing the divine" would be a disturbing sign of grandiosity. Some Christian traditions in particular have resisted any such notion, and have, at official level at least, consistently

---

30. I think I recall Kenneth Bailey making this point in addresses I heard in the mid-1990s. From whatever source, others have heard similar tales.
31. Ramshaw, *Treasures*, 370.

opted for language of ministers "equipping the ministry of all," rather than representing others, and less so again of representing God or Christ. In such a view, the presumption to represent Christ is understood to "tend . . . to lead implicitly to the idea that there can be only one minister in a congregation,"[32] whereas a stress on something like the "priesthood of all believers" is supposed to pull against any such supposed elitism. Understandings which emphasize the priesthood of all believers also raise important questions about what other implicit understandings might be in play in pastoral scenarios, in which quite apart from a minister's self-understanding and theological convictions, however sound or not, she is *perceived by others* as *in one way or another* representing Christ or God. In pastoral situations, what the notion of representing Christ entails cannot be determined by reference to the minister's understanding apart from other considerations, however theologically correct a minister may understand herself to be. And notably, whatever their possible reserve about the idea of ordained ministers representing Christ, some still do refer to their ministers as "reverend" and many ministers in those traditions still opt to wear clerical collars, as well as, say, preaching robes or banns. A notable example of a bolder approach, however, is the Uniting Church in Australia which upholds the notion of a minister of Holy Communion representing Christ, not only encouraging the presiding celebrant in the sacrament to enact the institution narrative, but using the language of representation forthrightly in its theologies of ministry and ordination. Note, for example:

> A ministry of leadership within the community will often need to be understood as a "representative" leadership. The new status into which a minister has been placed by ordination means that the Presbyter or Deacon may stand on behalf of the community before others, or before the Congregation itself, as a representative of the wider Church. The minister presiding at the Eucharist represents not only the local Congregation (both those present and those absent) who together celebrate the

---

32. Andrew D. Mayes, *Spirituality in Ministerial Formation: The Practice of Prayer* (Cardiff: University of Wales Press, 2009), 64.

sacrament, but the universal Church at all times and places which joins us "with choirs of angels and the whole creation in the eternal hymn." In another liturgical sense, the minister may represent Christ, although all Christians share that responsibility. At other times, the presence of a Presbyter or Deacon anywhere may symbolize the presence of the Church catholic in what God is doing in the world.[33]

Nevertheless to whatever extent a pastoral caregiver may perceive herself as a representative, even where formal call, commission, charge, or appointment are lacking, a Christian's understanding of herself as a part of the body of Christ, belonging together with others, and related to Christ Jesus, will constrain her sense of caring simply as an individual and will nurture her sense of always representing more than merely personal presence, crucial though that is.

Yet as a representative person, the Christian pastoral caregiver is also a public figure, and her work is beyond as well as among the Christian assembly. This is true especially of those called to ordination—not least because they undergo a significant public rite of admission into their orders—but it is also true of all persons who minister with any kind of commission from the church, in other specified ministries and in other ways. Hence, in many traditions, ordination services begin with a clear echo of the baptism services themselves:

> In baptism we are claimed by God,
> and given the gift of the Holy Spirit
> that we may live as witnesses to Jesus Christ
> and share his ministry in the world.[34]

This is a very strong statement, and intentionally so. It should not be underestimated. Its force is that *all* persons who exercise any ministry in the church do so primarily on the basis of their baptism. All persons

---

33. Robert Bos and Geoff Thompson, eds., *Theology for Pilgrims: Selected Theological Documents of the Uniting Church in Australia* (Sydney: Uniting Church Press, 2008), 363.
34. http://assembly.uca.org.au/worship/resources/order-service-in-church.html.

who exercise any ministry in the church do so not simply on their basis of personal initiative, but as an expression of baptismal witness. They represent the baptized, and are sharing the ministry of Christ.

## Public Symbols

Ordination is a major public symbol, which is why it takes place in the presence of a congregation. When an ordained person is inducted to a new placement, not only clergy or representatives of other churches and faiths may be present, but also representatives of many other local institutions. Such ritual practices help to locate the minister amidst a symbolic matrix, as herself a symbol; but whether or not such ritual scenes nurture this sense, as we have seen, the pastor is always a symbol.

In ways that a minister cannot always herself control, many other symbols attach around her. Two of the most obvious are the use of the prefix "reverend" and the use of the clerical collar, both deeply ambiguous. Yet it might be argued that these symbols also have public currency and that they may at least sometimes serve to allow the ministry of representative Christians to be received beyond the confines of congregational activity. It is important to appreciate that many things about a minister take on significance greater than her personal choices, simply by virtue of her role. Quite apart from the clerical collar, other kinds of clothing take on further symbolic meaning when worn by a minister. At a meeting recently, I was present alongside two other ministers from different areas in the city of Sydney. One, a minister on the prosperous area, wore a Ralph Lauren sweater, with a visible logo identifying it as such. Another, a minister in the relatively disadvantaged district, which hosts a thriving arts scene, sported a waistcoat and Doc Marten boots. Whether or not either of them was also wearing a clerical collar, their clothing symbolized an affinity, an inculturation, into their particular local community. A clerical collar might have identified them as a representative Christian, but their other clothing identified them within the cultural milieu of their neighborhood, and as such was being "used" in ministry, accompanied by more traditional symbols or not. It might be particularly demanding to determine the reception of symbols most closely associated with the person in particular—literally embodied in the sense that they are worn, and adorn; but many other symbols—like words—are riddled with ambiguities. The car a minister may drive takes on a significance greater than her personal preferences, simply by virtue of her role: If a minister travels in a two-seater sports car, that says something different from a minister who drives a minivan. If the sports car is evidently expensive, a further message is delivered.

Simply by virtue of being a minister, a minister is a symbol. A minister who fails to grasp this essential dynamic is quite unlikely to be effective in the public witness to which the church calls persons. Even where attempts are made to jettison symbolic dimensions of pastoral roles—as in contemporary casualness—it remains that the symbolic resonances of the role cannot entirely be shaken off. So Lathrop offers the important reminder that when the pastor is known by her or his first name—"'Pastor Sue,' 'Father Jim,' 'Reverend Mike,' or even just 'Sue' or 'Jim' or 'Mike'"—even then, "this symbolic use points towards a longing for intimacy."[35] It remains that "it is the pastor—the sign of wider connection, of God—who is spoken to as if to an intimate friend or family member." Even as "the pastor is often admitted to a place of closeness; the pastor must know that this place is symbolic, mediated." Exercising ministry from this mediated space is a constant and strenuous demand on all who represent the church, for as Sarah Coakley remarks, ministers'

> representative function may rightly remain somewhat invisible and untheorized: as has been sagely remarked by the anthropologist of religion Catherine Bell, the ritual actor is effective precisely if and when unconscious forces are released, and that is why there is a limit to the analysis that can take place.[36]

---

35. Lathrop, *Pastor*, 12. The following paragraph quotes from page 12 of Lathrop's book.
36. Sarah Coakley, "Prayer, Place and the Poor," in *Praying for England: Priestly Presence in Contemporary Society*, ed. Samuel Wells and Sarah Coakley (London: Continuum, 2008), 4.

## Shifting Symbols

A crucial point to emerge here is that the symbols are not static, they are constantly shifting, overlapping, interacting; and they may oftentimes be opaque, even to those who employ, offer, or seek to align themselves to them. Hence, Lathrop's stress on the pastor's constant relearning of Christian symbols and of her own role as a symbol, being "thrown together" with other symbols. The inherently unsettled aspect of symbolic mediation means at least that the pastor, as symbol, is not the sole determiner of the meaning of the symbol that she is. It is into this setting that the pastor brings herself in the difficult role she embraces. And if that point leads directly to the focus of the following chapter, this one should assert that the very instability, fluidity, and mess of symbols may itself be a gift to the mission of the church. In their instability, symbols may have wide meanings for different people as they engage with them. For example, perhaps only a regular, active congregational member would appreciate the fuller stretch of shepherding imagery in the ordination, funeral, and eucharistic rites of the church, but they may sense, if fleetingly and inchoately, that the pastoral caregiver can be a "gathering place for communal encounter with wider meaning" and make their own sense of the symbols the pastor places, carefully, with expectation, in public realms.

## Episcopal Church Explorations

What does this mean in The Episcopal Church? The remainder of this chapter offers an intensive exploration of ministries in the context of the Baptismal Covenant that marks the Book of Common Prayer.[37] It is one way to explore the contention made in my introduction that representative dynamics are learned in the liturgy.

In The Episcopal Church, congregational reaffirmation of baptism includes the Baptismal Covenant, itself the response to baptism and confirmation. Significantly, this commitment is in a form widely used by

---

37. In this section, I draw and build upon Stephen Burns and Bryan Cones, "A Prayer Book for the Twenty-first Century?" *Anglican Theological Review* 96 (2014): 639–60.

Christians across the world, and in many different traditions, so in that respect it plays a role in representing the church's catholicity. An emphasis on baptismal ecclesiology is a major mark of ecumenical liturgical renewal,[38] which is one reason why the texts of the Baptismal Covenant have themselves come to be used in many traditions across the world. In this congregational reaffirmation, persons are asked to repeat their own promises, made at baptism and confirmation, once more pledging themselves to Christ's ministry in the world:

*Celebrant*  Do you believe in God the Father?
*People*  I believe in God, the Father almighty,
creator of heaven and earth.
*Celebrant*  Do you believe in Jesus Christ, the Son of God?
*People*  I believe in Jesus Christ, his only Son, our Lord.
He was conceived by the power of the Holy Spirit
and born of the Virgin Mary.
He suffered under Pontius Pilate,
was crucified, died, and was buried.
He descended to the dead.
On the third day he rose again.
He ascended into heaven,
and is seated at the right hand of the Father.
He will come again to judge the living and the dead.
*Celebrant*  Do you believe in God the Holy Spirit?
*People*  I believe in the Holy Spirit,
the holy catholic Church,
the communion of saints,
the forgiveness of sins,
the resurrection of the body,
and the life everlasting.

---

38. For excellent introductions, see, from an Anglican perspective, Louis Weil, *A Theology of Worship* (New York: Church Publishing, 2000), 1–28, and from a Roman Catholic slant, Paul Philibert, *The Priesthood of the Faithful: Key to a Living Church* (Collegeville, MN: Liturgical Press, 2005), 56–73.

| | |
|---|---|
| *Celebrant* | Will you continue in the apostles' teaching and fellowship, in the breaking of bread, and in the prayers? |
| *People* | I will, with God's help. |
| *Celebrant* | Will you persevere in resisting evil, and, whenever you fall into sin, repent and return to the Lord? |
| *People* | I will, with God's help. |
| *Celebrant* | Will you proclaim by word and example the Good News of God in Christ? |
| *People* | I will, with God's help. |
| *Celebrant* | Will you seek and serve Christ in all persons, loving your neighbor as yourself? |
| *People* | I will, with God's help. |
| *Celebrant* | Will you strive for justice and peace among all people, and respect the dignity of every human being? |
| *People* | I will, with God's help.[39] |

The first part of the Baptismal Covenant is simply the Apostles' Creed, a fourth-century expression of Christian faith in a basic Trinitarian frame. The second part of the text—what Jeffrey Lee calls the "so what" questions[40]—sets alongside the ancient creedal expression of belief an account of Christian behaviors: worship, repentance, proclamation, service, and action for justice. The questions intend to articulate the practical consequences of the faith acknowledged by use of the creed. The form of these questions was new to the 1979 prayer book. Yet the form is not altogether innovative, in that the series of questions is an intentional expansion of a shorter Reformation-era text. In the English prayer book of 1662, the Apostles' Creed is followed by a single question: "Wilt thou then obediently keep God's holy will and commandments, and walk in the same all the days of thy life?" What we find in 1979 is a contemporary elaboration of this, stretched across five interrelated areas of practice.

---

39. *Book of Common Prayer*, 304–5.
40. Jeffrey Lee, *Opening the Prayer Book* (Cambridge, MA: Cowley, 1999), 80.

The Book of Common Prayer's baptismal resources are often said to be a major building block of the theology of the book. Ruth Meyers, for example, suggests that "widespread use of the baptismal covenant suggests that a baptismal ecclesiology is indeed taking root in the Episcopal Church."[41]

The baptismal service of the Book of Common Prayer has many notable features, some perhaps revolutionary. James Turrell suggests no less than that the prayer book makes "a stunning reversal of traditional Anglican thought"[42] because it displaces the traditional role of confirmation in its affirmation that "Holy Baptism is full initiation by water and the Holy Spirit into Christ's body the Church."[43] The Book of Common Prayer moves prayers and actions traditionally used in Anglican *confirmation* services (such as the laying-on-of-hands, and chrismation) into the context of *baptism*.[44] And while the full implication of the affirmation that all baptized people are fully initiated—that each newly baptized person, adult, child, or infant, would from then on share in Holy Communion—has not always been accepted and realized, it remains that the prayer book vision is startling in the context of the Anglican tradition. It is also a vision that has been compelling to other Anglicans, and indeed the Book of Common Prayer should be seen as marking the beginning of a sea change in Anglican practice.

One mark of this has been the way in which a specific and distinctive part of the BCP baptism service has migrated around the Anglican Communion. This confirms that the Baptismal Covenant has not only taken root in The Episcopal Church itself but also as it were branched out far and wide. For example, following closely behind the Book of Common Prayer of 1979, the Anglican Church of Canada produced a *Book of Alternative Services* in 1985 and simply incorporated the Book

---

41. Ruth A. Meyers, *Continuing the Reformation: Re-envisioning Baptism in the Episcopal Church* (New York: Church Publishing, 2000), 229.
42. James F. Turrell, *Celebrating the Rites of Initiation: A Practical Ceremonial Guide for Clergy and Other Liturgical Ministers* (New York: Church Publishing, 2013), 7. See also Meyers, *Continuing the Reformation*, 226.
43. *Book of Common Prayer*, 298.
44. Turrell, *Celebrating the Rites of Initiation*, 14.

of Common Prayer's Baptismal Covenant.[45] Other churches have made a more selective appropriation of the text. For example, in a book published over thirty years after the BCP 1979, Dwight Zscheile uses the "so what" questions as a key to his proposals for "renewing Episcopal identity."[46] He suggests that they are a "blueprint for discipleship," relating them to a range of contemporary evangelistic challenges and much else.

Indeed, the Baptismal Covenant can itself be seen as an assertion that worship is missional, as it is so central to the formation of new believers in readiness for baptism. As The Episcopal Church has retrieved forms of the catechumenate[47]—in this once more, with many Protestant traditions, following Roman Catholic initiative[48]—the Apostles' Creed is presented to candidates in the process, before they recite it at baptism.[49] It is part of the gift that is shared by the church with new believers, and the "so what" questions invite people into more than doctrinal understanding, head or even heart knowledge, but into ways of living, a shape of life. The promises of the Baptismal Covenant, as the Latin for "promise," *pro-missum*, reminds, are "before mission," even "for mission."[50]

One very strong mark of the Baptismal Covenant is its orientation to the world, its affirmation of the ministry of the baptized in the wider world outside the Christian assembly. This emphasis is of enormous and abiding importance, as, for sure, "*Liturgical rites are not the*

---

45. *Book of Alternative Services* (Toronto: Anglican Book Centre, 1985), 158–59.

46. Dwight J. Zscheile, *People of the Way: Renewing Episcopal Identity* (New York: Church Publishing, 2012), 89–100.

47. See the *Book of Occasional Services* (New York: Church Publishing, 1994), 113-30.

48. See the Roman Catholic *Rite of the Christian Initiation of Adults* (Chicago, IL: Liturgy Training Publications, 1988) and Protestant appropriations in, for example, the Uniting Church in Australia's *Uniting in Worship 2* and the Evangelical Lutheran Church in America's *Evangelical Lutheran Worship* (Minneapolis, MN: Augsburg Fortress Press, 2006).

49. *Book of Occasional Services*, 128. Note important reflections on the significance of the catechumenate in Louis Weil, "Baptism and Mission," in *Growing in Newness of Life: Christian Initiation in Anglicanism Today*, ed. David R. Holeton (Toronto: Anglican Book Centre, 1993), 74–79.

50. For this and many other good points about the links between baptismal commitments and mission, see Eileen D. Crowley, "Making More Visible Our Invisible Baptismal Promises," *Proceedings of the North American Academy of Liturgy—2011* (Notre Dame: NAAL, 2011), 93.

*whole of the church's public life*."[51] The sacraments themselves affirm a worldliness—the goodness of creation, the grace of things commonly used and needed outside the assembly: water, food, touch—as does an Anglican understanding of the gospel, which treasures the doctrine of the incarnation.[52] So it is good that the thrust of the Baptismal Covenant turns worshipers to the wider world which God loves and in which God's presence is to be celebrated. It is a dynamic of Christian worship that attention to central things of the liturgy—God's word, Christ's sacraments—turns attention to wide concerns.[53] At the same time, however, the Baptismal Covenant might also be thought to have implications for time and experience in Christian assembly. Indeed, it is surely crucial to imagine these implications. Guarding against creeping clericalism will mean looking out for "patterns of liturgical prayer in which that corporate identity is obscured, or in which one ministry is implicitly elevated above others so that the mutuality of ministry is eroded,"[54] and particularly being alert to any exaggeration of the status of the clergy while devaluing or patronizing laity.[55]

It can be helpful to have this dynamic understanding of roles in the liturgy when coming to the Book of Common Prayer opening gambit that "in all services, the entire Christian assembly participates in such a way that the members of each order within the Church, lay persons, bishops, priests and deacons, fulfill the functions proper to their respective orders, as set forth in the rubrical directions for each service."[56] It is, however, sometimes questionable how coherent these rubrics are with the notion of full participation by all the assembly, given certain tasks are inexplicably reserved to the ordained. William Seth Adams ably

---

51. Weil, *Theology of Worship*, 13 (italics in the original).
52. Louis Weil, "The Gospel in Anglicanism," in *The Study of Anglicanism*, ed. Stephen Sykes and John Booty (London: SPCK, 1998), 78.
53. Cf. David F. Ford, *The Shape of Living: Spiritual Disciplines for Daily Life* (London: Fount, 1997), 20.
54. Weil, *Theology of Worship*, 3–4.
55. Fredrica Harris Thompsett, *We Are Theologians: Strengthening the People of God* (New York: Church Publishing, 2004), 97.
56. *Book of Common Prayer*, 13.

identifies how the Book of Common Prayer's Baptismal Covenant is sometimes at odds with its clericalizing rubrics. There is an "entanglement" of "two ideas at work" in the prayer book's conflicting theologies of ministry: an entanglement "due to the fact that at the time of publication, the church's thinking on ministry was undergoing reformation, moving from a view which would understand 'ministry' to mean 'ordained ministry' to a view which would treat 'ministry' as a much broader idea, one inclusive of the whole church." Adams is admirably clear that the two theologies of ministry entangled in the BCP are not always "compatible," and that it is "impossible" to describe the Book of Common Prayer's theology of ministry "as if it were a unified theology."[57]

To pursue the conflict Adams identifies is neither to call into question the venerable tradition of ordaining some but not all Christians, nor to appeal for a practice of lay presidency or other proposals that suggest that there is nothing distinctive about the ministries of ordained persons. But it is to invite renewed clarity about what tasks properly belong to the ordained, and how the ordained are imagined, and imagine their own ministries, amongst the ministries of all the baptized. It is certainly reasonable enough to hold that some tasks belong to some and not all—and the International Anglican Liturgical Consultation on the Eucharist makes a good point with humor when it asserts "not every baptized Christian should play the organ!"[58]—but it always needs to be remembered that while the ministry of the ordained may be distinctive, "so are the gifts that others bring to the common life of the community."[59]

Who is able and encouraged to participate in representative ministries such as announcing the gospel and sharing communion are undoubtedly important, but they remain ancillary to larger challenges to renew all the people's participation in liturgical action, to manifest in

---

57. William Seth Adams, *Moving the Furniture: Liturgical Theory, Practice, and Environment* (New York: Church Publishing, 1999), 35.

58. David R. Holeton, ed., *Our Thanks and Praise The Eucharist in Anglicanism Today* (Toronto: Anglican Book Centre, 1998), 281.

59. Weil, *Theology of Worship*, 20.

embodied ways that the assembly is the celebrant of the liturgy. Louis Weil, for example, encourages the recovery of what, at least in some places, for the best part of the first millennium had been a congregational—not simply presidential—gesture of eucharistic prayer: *All* of the people stand *orant*, hands raised around the altar.[60] Richard Giles even suggests a verbal introduction to this practice that a presider might use right before eucharistic prayer: "We invite you now to place your orders of service on the floor, and to raise your hands in the posture of prayer and thanksgiving adopted by the first Christians. In so doing we make the Great Thanksgiving the prayer of the holy community of God's priestly people: no longer my prayer, but *our* prayer."[61] Where such an invitation is followed, many raised hands offer a powerful depiction that the Eucharist is consecrated by the prayer of the entire assembly, not the "magic hands" of the priest. And when we recall that the *orant* gesture in fact has a dual meaning deep in the Christian tradition—it gestures thanksgiving, as in many scriptural pericopes, but also, as Christians in early centuries came to emphasize, it sculpts the body in sacrifice, with hands held as if pinned up on a cross—we may find an even deeper, Christ-centered, experience of participation in the prayer.[62]

The Episcopal Church's Baptismal Covenant is an as yet underexplored resource for ministry—the ministry of all the baptized, in which pastors have distinctive roles. In its assertion that baptism is a—if not the—key symbol of ministry, it calls for a reframing of much inherited thought about ordination.

---

60. Louis Weil, *Liturgical Sense: The Logic of Rite* (New York: Seabury, 2012), 24, 61.
61. Richard Giles, *Creating Uncommon Worship: Renewing the Liturgy of the Eucharist* (Norwich: Canterbury Press, 2004), 162.
62. See further, Stephen Burns, *Liturgy*, SCM Studyguide (London: SCM Press, 2006), 58.

# CHAPTER 5

# The Person as Pastor

Dare to
declare
who you
are. It
isn't
far from
the shores
of silence
to the
boundaries
of speech.
The road
is not
long but
the way
is deep.
And you
must not
only
walk there,
you must
be prepared
to leap.[1]

---

1. Nicola Slee, *Praying Like a Woman* (London: SPCK, 2004), 60.

Nicola Slee's "Conversations with Muse" is sketched down the page like waves on the shoreline, as if visually to make the point that it keeps washing to shore with new challenges. What are readers dared to declare? Their Christian witness? their "coming out," "gay and proud"? either/or, both/and, and more? The poem may mean many things to its readers, as they bring their different experiences to it. In this chapter, we peruse a range of experience that is relevant to the caregiver's engagement with others, focusing on two in particular—ethnicity and gender—and drawing to a close with reflection on the spirituality of the pastoral carer. In keeping with the personal focus on which this chapter turns (even as it is juxtaposed to discussion of representative dimensions of ministry in the previous chapter), I discuss aspects of my own personal experience, to do with what John Vincent depicts as "blood" and "bread": blood—family, race, gender, sexuality, psychology; bread—location, livelihood, dependencies, socioeconomic status, and so on.[2]

## The Centrality of Experience

As earlier chapters have explored, much pastoral theology—perhaps especially in its therapeutic mode—is methodologically distinct from some other theological styles by its particular insistence on the centrality of experience. It must be recognized, however, that while commonly asserting the centrality of experience in theology, pastoral theologians do not agree about how experience is defined, articulated, and analyzed. Classical and liberationist responses to the therapeutic tradition make that point. Beyond the discipline of pastoral theology, other kinds of theologians can also view an emphasis on experience with considerable suspicion. At its most extreme, understandings of theology that limit divine revelation to scripture (as some Christians claim) are likely to be quite mistrustful of any move to concentrate attention on human experience—which may be seen as detracting from the source (scripture) in which God's reliable self-giving is understood to reside. Likewise ways

---

2. John Vincent, "An Urban Hearing for the Church," in *Gospel from the City*, ed. John Vincent and Chris Rowland (Sheffield: Urban Theology Unit, 1999), 115.

of thinking that emphasise the internal coherence of points of doctrine in an ordered "system" (systematic theology), which is understood to unfold in orderly procession through themes like God, Christ, Spirit, creation, human being, redemption, and church may regard an emphasis on experience as mistakenly open to sources outside the system, and vulnerable to inchoate mess (especially if the system itself accents human sinfulness). So in even stronger ways than the classical tradition seeks to correct the therapeutic tradition, different styles of pastoral theology may be dismissed as sociology or some other descriptor intended to exclude them from a supposed understanding of theology proper. An example may be seen in the writing of Alan Torrance, who is disparaging about the possibilities of "contextual theology," with which therapeutic and liberationist traditions of pastoral theology are in different and related ways aligned. A Scot, Torrance writes:

> if the symbols of Scottish culture are taken to be its indige-
> nous, national drink (whisky), its national recipe (the haggis)
> and its famously indigenous musical instrument (the bagpipes),
> this would seem to suggest that indigenous, Scottish theology
> should be characterized by spirit, guts . . . and large quantities
> of wind.[3]

In the context of reflections on the creedal clause "of one substance with the Father" he notes that the Christologies of many indigenous and contextual theologians "have little interest in affirming the *homoousion*," but rather seek to "to reinterpret Jesus's significance in the light of the spiritualities and conceptualities of their specific contexts." Referring to examples from "southern and eastern Asia, from the very different contexts of Sri Lanka, India, China, the oppressed workers (*min-jung*) of South Korea, and the peasant farmers of Japan and Thailand; in Australian 'indigenous theologies' Australiasian (sic) and in North America," he claims that "the irony of the situation illustrated in these

---

3. Alan Torrance, "Being of One Substance with the Father," in *Nicene Christianity: The Future for a New Ecumenism*, ed. Christopher Seitz (Grand Rapids, MI: Brazos Press, 2001), 231, note 2. The following paragraphs quote from pages 50–51 of Torrance's chapter.

contexts is precisely how unindigenous the self-conscious, identity-driven search for an indigenous theology is." Of particular interest in this present context is, perhaps, his suggestion that "identity" is an "archetypically Western concern," a point not without force, and one he connects to "conditioning" by "psychotherapeutic categories of self-affirmation." Torrance regards such contextual theology as "often the betrayal of the unselfconscious hard-nosed engagement with the question of what can be affirmed truthfully about God and God's engagement with human beings in all their diversity," and commends "steadfast focus on the truth question." In his own resistance to listening to the basic arguments of contextual theologians, in all their diversity—he disregards them all—he is surprisingly intemperate. Perhaps ironically for reflections on incarnation, he seems insensitive to some very obvious questions that confront his own approach. Of course, pastoral theologies themselves will accept little of Torrance-like lines of argument, and while ready to acknowledge the "messiness" of their discipline, also reassert their possibly messy methods in resistance either to theologies confined to scriptural or systematic parameters.

What many pastoral theologies might regard as uniting them is something like an insistence on the importance of "consistently insist[ing] upon the crucial nature of concrete experience in the generation of pastoral theology."[4] One way or another, if to different extents in different styles, contemporary experience has to be acknowledged in pastoral theology; it is not enough to speak of what may or may not have been the case in the experience of biblical figures, and it is not enough to speculate abstractly on unspecified, general experience. And in retort to systematic theologians especially, pastoral theologians are often interested in tracing the effects of concrete experience on all styles of theology, whether or not others wish to reflect upon their own experience. Nor is biblical interpretation unaffected by the experience of interpreters, and systems may to different extents reflect the experience of those

---

4. Emmanuel Y. Lartey, *Pastoral Theology in an Intercultural World* (Cleveland, OH: Pilgrim Press, 2006), 37.

who propose (or claim to explicate "given") systems. Unless experience is in conscious and critical play with theological interpretation and construction, pastoral theologians are unlikely to assume constructive theology to be sound. At their best, pastoral theologies manifest a "resolute . . . refus[al] to engage in theoretical discourse that fails to engage unpleasant or inconvenient aspects of human life."[5]

## The Trickiness of Experience

This being said, pastoral theologies can be deeply concerned to recognize that experience can be tricky to narrate and describe, and even to acknowledge, let alone analyze, define, categorize, and articulate in a way that can easily be understood by other persons. This is to say at least that experience may or may not be *reflective* experience, engaged consciously. It is *careful* reflection on experience that pastoral theologies attempt to evoke. At the same time, they may—as in the liberationist tradition—stress that personal experience is always part of larger dynamics that involve many others and shared ideas, if not always also others' embodied presence. Indeed, whether or not spoken aloud, any experience is necessarily to some extent shared, dependent upon, shaped by, powerful social forces, and not least in terms of what experience is widely, for better or worse, considered to count as "normal." As Dorothee Soelle puts it: "Every immediacy is mediated," and "by mediated I mean what is performed through education, tradition, language, and the domain of images or, as in the now normative mediation of the world through technology, what they exclude, prohibit, and define as an aberration or psychic malady."[6]

Making sense of experience may take time, and finding some language that seems adequate to it may take even longer. For all these reasons, it may take great patience, not to say courage, to arrive at a point of "daring to declare" who one is.

---

5. Lartey, *Pastoral Theology*, 91.
6. Dorothee Soelle, *The Silent Cry: Mysticism and Resistance* (Minneapolis, MN: Fortress Press, 2001), 53.

## The Caregiver's Experience

Pastoral theology's commitment to recognition of human experience calls pastoral carers to offer attention to others—as care-seekers—and *always also to themselves*—as caregivers. We may recognize, and come to recognize evermore deeply, different kinds of experience that affect who one is as a pastoral caregiver. The following pages invite readers to contemplate three particular arenas of experience: personal experience that one might readily recognize as significant in shaping one as a pastoral caregiver; experience of one's gender, ethnicity, and dimensions of one's personhood that shape one's place in wider culture; and the particular kind of Christian spirituality one embraces and which one brings to new experience.

In the first place, then, are particular encounters that we feel to shape a call, determination, and actual practices of care. In my case, a cluster of closely mediated experiences are central to my response to a call to Christian ministry, particularly to a ministry in which pastoral care would be central. One such experience was, in my early teenage years, having a friend who contracted cancer and subsequently underwent the amputation of his leg. The church that we both at the time attended with our parents was in the Open Brethren tradition, and so had no ordained leaders, and appointed no pastors. The elders—all men—had no training in either theology or pastoral practice, and had neither vision nor ability to respond well to the experience of the boy with cancer. At the time, it was striking to me that on a school visit (with my religious education class, which was making a sequence of Sunday visits to local worshiping communities) to a local congregation of the Church of England, my friend was named in prayer. The worship in the Brethren community, focused on either "the breaking of bread," a simple Eucharist, or "gospel service," an evangelistic preaching meeting, had no place for intercession—although there was a midweek prayer meeting, albeit not pastorally or locally focused. I was stunned to discover that the local Anglican church remembered my friend in prayer because every liturgy involved intercession, not only on Sundays, but also in smaller gatherings for daily prayer. Not only that, the priests of the community had been regular visitors to my friend's family at home. These things, quite small in themselves, were major revelations to me, opening up clear alternatives to the way in which my own family's religious community had coped with this particularly traumatic experience of illness. I have no doubt that this episode was a significant one among a larger number that led soon afterward to my own move into a Christian community with recognized leaders and appointed caring persons; but also the beginning of my conviction, which it did not take too long to articulate, that communities *need* appointed caring persons, and hence a kind of putting myself forward for the role.

Another significant experience for me followed closely on my friend's sickness with cancer. My grandfather suffered a severe stroke that left him badly paralyzed and unable to speak for the last nine years of his life. A formerly very active man, who loved the outdoors and spent much of his retirement walking and working his garden, was immobilized, confined to a geriatric ward of a local hospital, dependent on others for his most basic needs, and able to communicate only with the words "yes" and "no" (so that much "conversation" was reduced to questions) and through tears—sometimes, it seemed, from his intense frustration. My grandmother's devotion was unstinting, visiting him every single day, and the extended family was tested, sometimes painfully, in the challenges of enabling her to make her daily visits, quite apart from the challenges of sustaining regular visiting of their own. My immediate family visited on Sunday afternoons, which left me with no feeling of wishing to bring Sundays to a close with what was called the young people's fellowship, a meeting for praise and Bible study. My own experience of being close to my grandfather's illness, alongside my friend's illness, initiated me into a more ambiguous relationship to God. It was a relationship of struggle, not abandonment, in that in leaving the young people's fellowship, I did seek out another Christian group for young people in another church that met midweek. Yet some of my sense of struggle was no doubt from my experience with my grandfather in the hospital ward. One striking example was a visit, during one festive season, by a choir from a local church. No doubt well intentioned, they nevertheless entered the ward singing carols, wished everyone a merry Christmas, and left. What they did not see was a large room full of adults weeping, perhaps, I imagine, in recognition that the season did not promise much joy for them, perhaps because they could not leave, as the cheerful singers had so quickly done themselves. The choir made no personal engagement with the patients on the ward, nor did any visiting at other times, of which I was aware. Albeit well meaning, they were hapless. But for me, this very particular episode was another that I would later recognize as shaping a call to ministry that would involve a pastoral care as a central dimension, a centrality that had been lacking in much of the early teenage experience I have sketched. In these stories, which in my own case are the beginnings of two foundational narratives for many others in which a call culminates and was discerned, there was a lack of presence (in the Brethren elders), a hapless presence (in the choir), and what I experienced as a surprising, more gracious presence (in the intercession and visiting ministry of a local church). No deep points can or should be drawn deductively on the basis of these narratives, but they do unfold into a much bigger picture of a personal conviction that I would myself be involved in pastoral care.

In the second place are sometimes difficult to face experiences of gender, ethnicity, sexuality, bodily (dis-)ability, and other aspects of identity, inherited and/or chosen, more or less concrete, but that always frame all our interactions. I am a white male who has lived in cultures in which white males have long been assumed (especially by white males) to be "normal" human beings. It might be thought that such a point hardly needs to be rehearsed, until, as just one example, it is recalled how in an earlier chapter's discussion of public theology feminists theologians charged others for neglect of women's perspectives. So it is worth impressing that the experience of white males has too often been assumed to be representative of all human beings, and that the experience of human beings who are not white males has too often not been regarded as being as important as that of white males. I therefore assume the power of pervasive dynamics of patriarchy in the cultures to which I have and do belong. I have come to think of myself—though only because of the company I have kept—as able to recognize some of the ways in which patriarchy is constantly reasserted and reinscribed into cultures and subcultures, and to lament and sometimes resist it. Two of the most important choices I have made, alongside the decision to be ordained, have been to marry my wife and to become a parent. These decisions tie me, by choice, in life commitments to other persons and to communities—in the case of marriage and parenthood, to very particular persons; in the case of ordination, to a innumerable community of Christian believers, some of whom to which I have particular accountabilities. Marriage and ordination are life vows, and in Roman Catholic tradition they are two of the seven sacraments—in fact, the two which usually exclude each other, as in Roman Catholic theology human beings can normally personally receive six of the seven sacraments, with reception of orders to the priesthood involving embrace of celibacy, and so not marriage, which bars one from the order of priests. Parenthood is a different kind of commitment, which in my case arises from marriage, and that beyond the official theology of the Roman Catholic tradition might well be regarded as sacramental, if by that one means an experience that conveys divine grace. At the present time, I am able-bodied, but conscious not least through closely mediated experience of my grandfather's illness, that this is, for all human persons, a fragile marker of identity, and may very well be temporary. In any case, the key point at this stage in our explorations is to impress that some aspects of our identity are sedimented, others are choices, and others again are shifting and may well change over time. Whatever, we are uniquely ourselves, and one's felt sense may not neatly match others who either look alike, articulate similar stories, or share related experiences. In the particular mixture of our human identity, we are, each one, complicated—remembering the Latin roots of "complicated" as suggesting the sense of "folding together": "We are a folding together (*com-plicatio*) not only of multiple roles and relationships, but also of multiple internal states of emotion and identity."[7] Or, simply put, in a sense we all have multiple selves.[8]

---

7. Pamela Cooper-White, "Com[l]plicated Woman: Multiplicity and Relationality across Gender and Culture," in *Women Out of Order: Risking Change and Creating Care in a Multicultural World*, ed. Jeanne Stevenson-Moessner and Teresa Snorton (Minneapolis, MN: Fortress Press, 2009), 9.
8. Anthony G. Reddie, *Is God Colour-blind? Insights from Black Theology for Christian Ministry* (London: SPCK, 2009), 41.

## The Complications of Personal Identity

To explore further insight into two particular—and most important—"complications," gender and ethnicity, I next distill the arguments of two theologians from whom I have learned, sketching some personal responses to their work, which I take to be appropriate to the nature of this chapter, and its themes. I do so in order to encourage the reader to do the same.

### Soskice on the Significance of Gender

Janet Martin Soskice is a Canadian teaching theology in Britain, and a Roman Catholic who, at the time she wrote some significant and startling pieces on gendered experience, was teaching in an Anglican theological college in Oxford. Her background is in biblical studies, but her teaching area is philosophical theology. Two short pieces on "women's problems?" and "just women's problems?" are both from the early 1990s and are juxtaposed in a collection, *Spiritual Classics from the Late Twentieth Century*. Their place in that collection itself suggests some strong estimation that they are significant pieces of reflection in their time. The section of the collection that focuses on Soskice's work accents a key theme throughout her writing: "God loves women." Soskice herself writes:

> Despite cowardly tendencies to trundle back to [other topics—like bible or philosophy], I feel a certain obligation to write on the topics of women and the Church, and women and ethics, [because] one day I feel God might ask of me, "You were there. You saw it. What have you done for these ones that I love?"[9]

Despite the fact that Soskice is a philosopher, both pieces are written in highly anecdotal mode. They are in large part reflections on particular experiences that together narrate her own growing awareness of the significance of "women's problems." She tells a story about a student who announced to her that the problems of her workplace having no

---

9. Janet Martin Soskice, "Just Women's Problems?" in *Spiritual Classics from the Late Twentieth Century*, ed. Ann Loades (London: Church House Publishing, 1995), 4.

crèche was "just a women's problem":[10] It had been assumed, even by women, that children were women's responsibility. Soskice tells of how, as a teacher of theology, she came to the sense that the Christian tradition has oppressed, silenced women:

> As one worked and lived in the theological college . . . one couldn't help, as a woman, being aware of working with texts and traditions and circumstances created by men with a male population in mind. . . . Somehow the barrage of ancient opinion, the structures into which one was perceived to fit oddly, the little niggling but perduring negatives, which one felt, in a place which fit the young male candidates like a glove, all conspired to make one feel that women were not really quite as good as men, that God didn't care about women quite as much as men, that women's sufferings (so many of them not even figuring on the ethics or pastoral courses) didn't matter quite as much as those of men.

And she writes of "one particularly grim day [when] I remember thinking, 'It doesn't matter, because God *loves* women!' and somehow, to my surprise . . . weep[ing] with relief." Amidst such anecdotes are confronting pieces of conceptual thinking. So patriarchy "does not mean that some men are nasty to women. . . . It is about the structures that have been created, over hundreds of years, in which men were the main determinants; structures that do not take women's lives into consideration" but in which men, and children, suffer as women do, if in different ways: "Women's problems" are *not* "just women's problems" because in one way or another all human beings are depleted and diminished by travail experienced by women. And it is not only men who may be patriarchal, as women too may well have imbibed the dynamics of patriarchy, "blind[ly], or even wilfully blind[ly]." Further, sexism "is not something that hurts women's feelings, sexism is something that kills millions and millions of girls and women each year," because women and girls are consistently the victims of "persistent failure to give girl children and

---

10. Sockice, "Just Women's Problems," 49–50. The following paragraphs quote from pages 49–58 of Soskice's essay.

women medical care similar to that which men get, the failure to give them comparable food to that which men get, and failure to provide equal access to what social services there might be."

Soskice evidences this in relation to hard statistics about mortality and infant-mortality rates in the so-called two-thirds world. So she argues that sexism needs to be seen in a bigger context than Europe and North America (and by implication "the West"). God's love for women needs to be shown in theology by "not forgetting" women's experience: by "not collud[ing] in silencing the already half-voiced and [by not] making the problems of women just women's problems," but by "mapping [women's] sufferings on the broken and risen body of Christ."

Soskice's reflections evoke strong responses in me, and indeed have shaped me deeply. Over time, parts of Soskice's argument have been enormously important to me—especially the insistence that feminist issues should not be trivialized, because they are *literally* a matter of life and death ("sexism is not something that hurts women's feelings"). Indeed, this conviction has become absolutely central to me.

I am also drawn to Soskice's use of anecdote, and it has helped to convince me that the narration of experience is a crucial mode of theology. Her own willingness, not least as a philosopher of religion, to employ anecdotes from her own experience, can be held as lending weight to emphases in the therapeutic tradition of pastoral theology. Anecdotes have authority—not least because they can undermine and explode abstract, systematic ideas that can be assumed to be, or asserted to be, certainties. Theology needs anecdotes in order to articulate the lived struggles of human experience.

### Beckford on Black and White

Robert Beckford, a black Pentecostal theologian of African-Caribbean heritage, wrote about whiteness in a book engendered by racialized rioting in the city of Birmingham, and that was later collected in a seminal reader on black theology. At the time of writing, Beckford was based in the University of Birmingham, teaching in its Department of Theology and Department of Cultural Studies. His orbit of influence has, however, long been much broader than academia, as he had also worked as a television presenter, producing and fronting programs on the interface of religion and culture, not least with respect to issues of ethnicity.

Beckford asserts that whiteness is about more than skin color, but also concerns worldview, social location, and behavioral characteristics.[11] Whiteness, he argues, is a cultural construction, which can even sometimes be used in black majority communities to denote privilege and superiority. As strange as it may sound, there is a sense, he suggests, in which black people can "become white" and so gain access to social advantage. The way to become white, however, is to *accommodate* to the majority white culture, which entails the sacrifice and denial of aspects of identity as a black person.

According to Beckford, whiteness has a number of characteristics. One is "invisibility": "Some white people tend not to see it," especially if they have no experience of being a minority or belonging to a minority group. Straight, white men often are the least sensitive and most offensive, incapable of seeing their whiteness. Whiteness is often not considered part of the cultural mix—as "multicultural" issues are regarded as *black* issues. Whiteness is "not racialized" and seen as "ethnically neutral," but may nevertheless operate strongly as a norm. So dominant cultural notions of, for instance, normality may be closely aligned to whiteness, as might notions of the best kind of exceptions to norms—for instance, the most beautiful. In this context, blackness can be seen as a different kind of—inferior kind of—exception to normality. One special problem is that these norms draw on Christian tradition for some of their energy, given that western theology has all too often correlated whiteness/fairness/light with goodness and with God. (This problem is deeply inscribed in the history of Bible translation, liturgical usage, and textual traditions).[12] So Christianity is part of the problem.

---

11. Robert Beckford, "Whiteness," in *Black Theology in Britain: A Reader*, ed. Michael N. Jagessar and Anthony G. Reddie (London: Equinox, 2007), 100. The following paragraphs quote from pages 100–103 of Beckford's essay.
12. On this point, see Michael Jagessar and Stephen Burns, *Christian Worship: Postcolonial Perspectives* (Sheffield: Equinox, 2011).

Like Soskice, Beckford makes his points with powerful anecdotes: On a television program, "Trading Races," a black person volunteers to be made-up as a white person and finds himself able to access all kinds of places he would not usually, and may well would not feel safe, as a person of an ethnic minority. And Beckford relates how he himself, arriving at a television studio one day, in suit and tie, was met by a receptionist who assumed that a white delivery person, in motorbike leathers, was the "expert" arriving to contribute to the academic discussion to which Beckford had been invited.

Another dimension of whiteness is an alliance with terror: Black people might literally fear for their lives when white politicians make detrimental statements about black people and black culture. Racial terror is real—it responds to real violence.[13] Another dimension, less acute but still damaging, is white appropriation of blackness. So white cultures "borrow" (steal) selectively from black cultures—clothes-style and music-style are common and obvious examples—in ways that represent a contemporary imperialism, in continuity with empire. But "credit and material reward is not given back to the black community."

A more positive dimension is antiracism. Whiteness, for Beckford, is "at its most significant" when it is associated with antiracism. He urges recognition that some white people have been involved in the like of fighting to free slaves, marching against fascists, and standing in solidarity with the suffering of black people. These memories need to be celebrated, he suggests, especially in churches.

Like Soskice's work on gender, Beckford's work on ethnicity evokes strong responses from me. My own life has been shaped by the city and the institutions in which Beckford has also lived and worked. Birmingham—where I moved in my early thirties—was the first place where I worshiped regularly in black majority churches and was the place of my own first regular experiences of being the only white person and one of very few white persons in large gatherings of black persons—therefore of being (briefly) an ethnic minority with a culture

13. Beckford, "Whiteness," 102.

marginal to the (immediate) norm. I worked in the institution where Beckford heard James Cone's call to study whiteness, and representing black theologies had become central to that institution, and in my time in Birmingham this was spearheaded by the like of Anthony Reddie, Mukti Barton, and Michael Jagessar. So for the first time in my life, I was experiencing daily, sustained critical scrutiny and expectation that what I was saying, teaching, praying, preaching, what we were singing, how we were acting was humanly inclusive. I enjoyed this challenge, and have continued to try to make it my own. The Queen's Foundation for Ecumenical Theological Education, Birmingham,[14] was the first context in which I engaged in any sustained listening to black experience. I hope that I have since become more sensitive to knowing what humanly inclusive theology might sound and read like. My time in Birmingham, was not, though, the first time I had been aware of racism—so that prior awareness is no doubt part of what made me willing and hopefully able to learn what I could in Birmingham. My first closely mediated experiences of racism were in fact in Australia, where I have Aboriginal relatives, and where I first became shocked and angry about the different ways I was treated when I was and when I was not with my Aboriginal relatives. I experienced firsthand how people spoke and acted differently toward me—and for me, of course, these experiences were brief ones, not daily, sustained, and ordinary. I also saw for myself the legacy of racism in public policy, the social attitudes that shape notions of "normality," and the interplay of Christian teaching and Christian institutions in these dynamics, in visiting my relatives' home in a central Queensland Aboriginal settlement. The place originated as a *forced* settlement, a highly controlled community, marked by very significant deprivation of freedom and self-determination (directly in terms of lack and/or "supervision" of money, and domestic arrangements, let alone other aspects of "opportunity" like access to social services, health care, and education), and that is still rightly described as both deprived and dysfunctional as a

---

14. See Stephen Burns, Nicola Slee, and Michael Jagessar, eds., *The Edge of God: New Liturgical Texts and Contexts in Conversation* (Peterborough: Epworth Press, 2008), for a range of essays relating to the Queen's Foundation.

result of racist attitudes and action against its inhabitants, past and present. My first *visits* to their *home* (so, again, my own experience was brief, not daily, sustained, and ordinary) also coincided with experience of ministry in Britain working with large numbers of asylum seekers newly arrived in the local area where I was parish priest. Part of my ministry often involved a weekly joint meeting with the local police and the local Interfaith Forum in which I was involved, to receive reports from local people from ethnic minorities (including many asylum seekers) of racist harassment, and very often racist violence. No week went by when there was no report. These experiences changed me, at least enough to know that confronting whiteness, including my own, is crucial.

These are experiences that I carry with me into pastoral scenarios, either as caregiver or care-seeker. How pastoral caregivers are engaged, thoughtfully or otherwise, wittingly or otherwise, with respect to gender and ethnicity—as other aspects of their "blood" and "bread"—shape their experience of pastoral care, both given and received. What we see in attention to Soskice and Beckford is that aspects of personal identity are deeply embedded in structural dynamics, social mores, and cultural codes, none of which are value-neutral, but value-laden, and that caregivers cannot afford to be insensitive to such factors.

Yet how caregivers respond to such challenges will differ, depending not least to their allegiance to therapeutic, classical, or liberationist traditions of pastoral theology. For liberationists at least, analysis of the sociopolitical dimensions of ethnicity and gender may result in perspectives like Shawn Copeland's, as she elaborates what she identifies as the structural oppression of patriarchal and in other ways unjust contexts. Copeland employs feminist rhetoric of "the master's house" to make her forceful theological point:

> The "master's house" is the metaphor for the institutionalization of heterosexist white racist supremacy. The domain of sin and evil is perpetuated by the interlocking structures of sexism, racism, homophobia, and acquisitive capitalism. In this house, intentionally or unintentionally, "reality is seen in the form of a hierarchy or pyramid." This is a place characterized by fear, self-regard and scramble for position. In this house, authority is

exercised from the top down; beliefs, meanings, values, and truth are promoted through domination and competition. Whoever questions this view of reality is undermined or ridiculed. Myths are fabricated to demonstrate the inferiority of those who live outside. Thus, the master's house is off limits to blacks, indigenous peoples, persons afflicted with AIDS, uppity women, Jews, Latinos, Asians, gays and lesbians, the poor and the needy; their critical perspectives are neither sought nor desired. Through aggression and the subjugation of persons, human community is mocked or destroyed. The tools that build and sustain this house include the suppression of new questions and insights; the separation of mind and body, thought and action; domination and control; exclusion and objectification of persons and nature.

God's household is set against the master's.[15]

Copeland is therefore a powerful ally of liberationist approaches to pastoral care, and she draws on the work of Letty Russell to identify several strategies for contesting the dynamics of "the master's house," all of which are relevant to the work of a pastor:

(1) seeking, encouraging, and welcoming fresh questions from those on the margin; (2) recovering the "dangerous memories" of those who have placed the authority of God's house above the powers and principalities of this world—foremothers and fore-sisters in particular; (3) acknowledging that social, ecclesiastical, and academic arrangements are shaped by finite, limited, local human decisions that can be changed in genuine encounter with new questions and needs; (4) recognizing that the liberal logic of token-inclusion is but a subtle tool of domination and control; (5) resisting the dualistic split of mind and body, thought from action, and rhetoric from behavior, and nurturing wholeness of living; (6) refusing the emulate the oppressor; and (7) searching

---

15. Shawn Copeland, "Journeying To the Household of God: The Eschatological Implications of Method in the Theology of Letty Mandeville Russell," in *Liberating Eschatology: Essays in Honor of Letty M. Russell*, ed. Margaret A. Farley and Serene Jones (Louisville, KY: Westminster John Knox Press, 1999), 39.

out and celebrating hints and clues of God's "coming towards us" in communities of faith and struggle.[16]

Copeland exemplifies a liberationist approach to theology more broadly, even as her vision is relevant to other pastoral theologies. And dense and demanding as her vision is, it might serve as an invitation to explore further the costliness of ministry that is identified with the underprivileged and among those subject to injustice.

## Personal Spirituality

Like the symbolic dimensions of the work of pastoral care, which is impressed upon pastoral caregivers by the Christian tradition and continuing Christian practice, "blood" and "bread" are also, and unavoidably, the human conditions in which we may come to have faith or embrace some sort of spirituality. In an overarching culture in which pastoral care is not necessary any longer associated with representative Christians (so hospitals, schools, shopping malls, and sports clubs, and other institutions and groups may now appoint pastoral or spiritual caregivers with no expressed commitments to Christian worshiping communities—let alone those who lead that worship), a willingness to be publicly identified as a person of a certain kind of spirituality may remain a central marker of a Christian pastoral caregiver.

The notion of spirituality is of course notoriously difficult to define, as I learned from noticing some more or less contemporary approaches emerging from the same place, indeed, same university department of theology: Stephen Barton suggests that "spirituality . . . has to do with the sense of the divine presence and living in the light of that presence. There are two basic aspects: . . . knowing and being known by God . . . and responding with the whole of life, . . ."[17] while Ann Loades turns her attention to the question of what may make a spirituality specifically Christian:

---

16. Copeland, "Journeying," 41.
17. Stephen Barton, *The Spirituality of the Gospels* (London: SPCK, 1992), 1.

If a spirituality is to be identifiably Christian . . . at some point or other, some form of connection with the Christian tradition will need to be discernible. Beyond that, perhaps we need only bear in mind that the "fruit of the Spirit" includes "love, joy, peace, patience, kindness, goodness, faithfulness, gentleness, self-control" (Galatians 5:22).[18]

Philip Sheldrake addresses the same concern:

If "spirituality" is not to embrace absolutely anything, we . . . need to ask what we mean by the word. "Christian spirituality" . . . refers to the ways in which the particularities of Christian belief about God, the material world and human identity find expression in basic values, lifestyles and spiritual practices.[19]

In light of the fact that pastoral care (as well as spiritual care) is oftentimes used without any specific reference to religious communities or practices, these clarifications of what (Christian) spirituality may mean are insightful. They are also a context to which specific practices of Christian prayer can be brought, as these deep traditions of such prayer can be regarded as offering clues as to what pastoral care might involve/has, in historical perspective, involved[20]: A so-called monastic/desert tradition of prayer especially treasures scripture and silence and attention to the interior landscape of human life, while a so-called cathedral/city tradition especially values the other-centered practice of praise, the public witness and visibility of the pray-er, and especially the sheer hard work of the tough discipline of intercession. Of course, these traditions also invite a folding together in any serious and patient attempt to represent the riches of the Christian tradition's wisdom about prayer. The point is, perhaps, to be "soaked" in prayer, as Sarah Coakley suggests in her essay on "Prayer, Place and the Poor," in which she invokes Evelyn Underhill's

---

18. Ann Loades, ed., *Spiritual Classics from the Late Twentieth Century* (London: Church House Publishing, 1995), v.

19. Philip Sheldrake, "Preface," in *New SCM Dictionary of Christian Spirituality*, ed. Philip Sheldrake (London: SCM Press, 2005), vii.

20. See Paul Bradshaw, *Two Ways of Praying: Introducing Liturgical Spirituality* (London: SPCK, 1995), for outlines of the "two ways of praying" sketched here.

insistence that "only a priest whose life is soaked in prayer, sacrifice, and love can, by his own spirit of adoring worship, help us to apprehend [God]."[21] Coakley elaborates in her own words, in such a way to draw out that such "soaking" is not merely personal, but is a public witness:

> Without the daily *public* witness of a clergy engaged, manifestly and accountably, alongside their people, in the disciplined, long-haul life of prayer, of ongoing personal and often painful transformation, the Church at large runs the danger of losing its fundamental direction and meaning.[22]

In their book *Practical Theology in Action*, on "Christian thinking in the service of church and society," Paul Ballard and John Pritchard make a commendable attempt to suggest "a spirituality equal to the task" of "practical ministry," a spirituality which "supports and nourishes"[23] such ministry. Given their emphasis on the society of which church is a part, their depiction of such a spirituality includes features which accent the social as well as ceremonial scenes of ministry. They suggest that a spirituality equal to the task of practical ministry will be "biblical and radical," "socially and politically earthed," "engaged with suffering and celebrating resurrection," have "depth and integrity," be "drawn to the image of journey," "humble," "value . . . narrative," "corporate," "mission-focused and ecumenical," and one of "celebration." Notably, however, they stop short of the kinds of liberationist advocacy—explicitly siding with the poor—that Stephen Pattison promotes, and they include only one woman's voice in the range of perspectives they commend.[24] It is not just that their vision may not be as "socially and politically aware and

---

21. Sarah Coakley, "Prayer, Place and the Poor," in *Praying for England: Priestly Presence in Contemporary Society*, ed. Samuel Wells and Sarah Coakley (London: Continuum, 2008), 7.

22. Coakley, "Prayer, Place and the Poor," 8.

23. Paul Ballard and John Pritchard, *Practical Theology in Action: Christian Thinking in Service of Church and Society* (London: SPCK, 2006), 178.

24. Ballard and Pritchard, *Practical Theology*, 177–91. Kathy Galloway is mentioned on pages 187 and 191.

committed" as alternatives like Pattison's, it is also that they may unwittingly or otherwise have excluded more public perspectives, if one mark of being public is the value of inclusivity.

Some of the marks of Ballard and Pritchard's spirituality are resonant with Emmanuel Lartey's account of "care-inspired faith."[25] While also open to the charge of depoliticizing pastoral care, Lartey provides some alternative suggestions for a spirituality adequate to the challenges of ministry. He draws out what he calls "features of theology that pastoral theologians particularly bring to the table out of their pastoral praxis," in which his stress is on "tentative," "provisional," "poetic," and "exploratory" modes of reflection, on the "enigmatic" God's "vulnerability" and "weakness," "elusive love," "mystery," "relation" to and "image" in human beings. Although not purporting to be about "spirituality" as such, Lartey's attention to the mood and tone of theological reflection in pastoral ministry is not only emphatically unsystematic but "remains a work in progress and can never be the final or complete word." Lartey is, however, adamant that "pastoral theologians are as interested in all other theologians in notions of the being, nature and activities of God." He elaborates, "The particular emphasis they bring to the theological task is the exploration of how concepts of God are related to pastoral practice," practice that is not merely "derived" from other "stronger" (systematic, historical) modes of theological thinking, which is then "applied." Pastoral theology, he avers, inspires "prayerful and humble interaction with God."

In my classes on pastoral theology, a tradition has grown of beginning each gathering with a period of extended silence for prayer, sometimes introduced by the psalm of the week in the Revised Common Lectionary (sometimes read in different translations), with the silence leading into a demanding and stretching litany from Uniting in Worship 2.[26] Notes about the litany suggest its roots in the English Book of

---

25. Emmanuel Y. Lartey, *Pastoral Theology for an Intercultural World* (Cleveland, OH: Pilgrim Press, 2006), 93–120. The following paragraph quotes from pages 103–20 of Lartey's book.
26. *Uniting in Worship 2* (Sydney: Uniting Church Press, 2005), 281–84.

Common Prayer of 1549, but its idiom is fresh and its range of attention to the contemporary world is wide. *Uniting in Worship 2* suggests that the litany "may be adapted for local situations and circumstances," but it is quoted here in full in its form in the book because, as it is, it depicts not only the kind of prayer in which pastoral caregivers may become immersed as they seek to represent God's work in the world, but because it also suggests something of the kind of "answer" to the prayer that the pastoral caregiver may herself need to become. When the pray-er prays "for those in need" and asks that God cares for the poor, welcomes the alienated, heals and comforts, has mercy, visits the lonely, she must realize that she is to be the least part of the answer to that very prayer.

O Lord our God,
you hear our prayers before we speak,
and answer before we know our need.
Although we cannot pray as we ought,
may your Spirit pray in us,
drawing us to you and toward our neighbors.
**Amen.**

We pray for the whole creation:
may all things work together for good,
until, by your design,
your children inherit the earth and order it wisely.
**Let the whole creation praise you, Lord our God.**

We pray for the Church of Jesus Christ;
that, begun, maintained and promoted by the Holy Spirit,
it may be true, engaging, glad, and active,
doing your will.
**Let the Church be always faithful, Lord our God.**

We pray for peace in the world.
Disarm weapons, silence guns,
and put out ancient hate that smolders still,
or flames in sudden conflict.

Create goodwill between every race and nation.
**Bring peace on earth, O God.**

We pray for enemies, as Christ commanded;
for those who oppose us or scheme against us,
who are also children of your love.
May we be kept from infectious hate
or sick desire for vengeance.
**Make friends of enemies, O God.**

We pray for those involved in world government,
in agencies of control or compassion,
who work for the reconciling of the nations:
keep them hopeful, and work with them for peace.
**Unite our broken world, O God.**

We pray for those who govern us,
for those who make and administer our laws.
May this country always be a land of free people
who welcome exiles and work for justice.
**Govern those who govern us, O God.**

*For those in need*

We pray for those who are poor, those who are hungry,
in need of employment, homes or education.
Increase in us, and in all who prosper,
concern for the disinherited.
**Care for the poor, O God.**

We pray for social outcasts;
for those excluded by their own aggression
or by the harshness of others.
May we accept those whom our world names unacceptable,
and so show your mighty love.
**Welcome the alienated, O God.**

We pray for sick people who suffer pain,
or struggle with demons of the mind,

who silently cry out for healing:
may they be patient, brave, and trusting.
**Heal the sick and troubled, O God.**

We pray for the dying, who face the final mystery:
may they enjoy light and life intensely,
keep dignity, and greet death unafraid,
believing in your love.
**Have mercy on the dying, O God.**

We pray for those whose tears are not yet dry,
who listen for familiar voices and look for familiar faces:
in their loss, may they affirm all that you promise in Jesus,
who prepares a place for us within your spacious love.
**Comfort those who mourn, O God.**

We pray for people who are alone and lonely,
who have no one to call in easy friendship:
may they be remembered, befriended,
and know your care for them.
**Visit lonely people, O God.**

We pray for people who do not believe,
who are shaken by doubt, or have turned against you.
Open their eyes to see beyond our broken fellowship
the wonders of your love displayed in Jesus of Nazareth,
and to follow when he calls them.
**Conquer doubt with faith, O God.**

We pray for families, for parents and children:
may they enjoy one another, honor freedoms,
and forgive as freely as we are all forgiven
in your huge mercy.
**Keep families in love, O God.**

We pray for young and old:
give impatient youth true vision,
and experienced age openness to new things.

Let both praise your name.
**Join youth and age together, O God.**

We pray for people everywhere:
may they come into their own as children of God,
and inherit the kingdom prepared in Jesus Christ,
the Lord of all and Savior of the world.
**Hear our prayers, almighty God,**
**in the name of Jesus Christ,**
**who prays with us and for us,**
to whom be praise for ever. Amen.

This does, I suggest, move pastoral caregivers toward a spirituality equal to the task of care that they embrace. As Don Saliers says, "intercessory prayer and the common prayer for others is, like the whole range of Christian liturgy, our 'school for ministry.' And our ministries must be the stuff of prayer."[27]

---

27. Don E. Saliers, *Worship and Spirituality* (Akron, OH: OSL Publications, 1996), 73.

# AFTERWORD: SEMINARY

In the pages of this book, various public settings have each been empha-sized as loci of ministry. Anton Boisen's vision of Clinical Pastoral Education took us to the hospital, Stephen Pattison's convictions in which streetlights, not bandages, are the pastor's focus, led us to think about road work. Both of these contexts challenge an individualistic approach to pastoral care and call attention to broader contexts. Feminist correctives to the therapeutic tradition—enlarging perspective from the living human document to the living human web—are just one of the criss-crosses, slopings, from one tradition to another, part of the tension and correction that can go on between them. I have said that other loci might have been added to hospital and road work, and what pastors can learn from Boisen and his care on psychiatric wards and from Pattison and his concern for "the politics of pastoral care" can be transferred to other public spheres: detention centers,[1] art galleries,[2] cafés. As part one, above, has suggested, pastoral care has wide settings, it has public dimen-sions. And at least some of the contours of public ministry can be traced through exploration of pastoral theology *emerging* from the therapeutic

1. See Susanna Snyder, *Asylum Seeking, Migration and Church* (Aldershot: Ashgate, 2012) for important work on this context, and moving reflections in *Bishops on the Border: Pastoral Responses to Immigration* (New York: Church Publishing, 2013).
2. See Jonny Baker, *Curating Worship* (New York: Church Publishing, 2010) and Mark Pierson, *The Art of Curating Worship* (Minneapolis, MN: Sparkhouse, 2011) for creative ideas about worship in public spaces, modeled on notions of curating.

tradition, *being nurtured* by a classical focus and *reframed* by liberationist emphases. Overly individualistic and overly churchly approaches to pastoral care can and should be challenged, not so that a personal emphasis is supplanted, but at least to ensure that it is supplemented.

At the same time, the ecclesial arena should never be forgotten as a locus of pastoral care. I have stressed not only gathering at the altar, in Christian assembly around word and sacrament, as a resource for pastoral care, but also that the altar is a place to where representative dynamics of ministry can be learned. Part two has proposed that pastoral care is always entangled in a symbolic milieu that, however much a pastoral caregiver can only be herself, also makes her "mythically more." These dynamics also invite attention to a wider than personal focus.

My explorations press the importance of linking this representative work more robustly to the public dimensions of ministry. The therapeutic tradition encourages hope and confidence that pastoral caregivers may indeed find a role beyond the liturgical arena, and what is more that they may do so in what may often be quite ambiguous space. Likewise, the classical tradition in its own turn is not concerned with any narrow sense of the gathered community, but with the community's identity as one *sent* as well as gathered (and the gathering has various sendings) in which leaders are responsible for the care of those who are not present at the gathering. The turnings of liturgical direction *within* the assembly—the presider's standing with the people as their representative, and facing the people as Christ's representative—have a part to play in helping presiders and others to learn their representative capacities *beyond* congregational life. I hope that it is obvious that the liberationist tradition is adamant not only that the sociopolitical contexts of ministry must be considered, but also that it offers resources with which those contexts can be critiqued and engaged with a view to changing them for the better. What the liberationist tradition underlines so forcefully is that the best ways to care may not be in reactive responses to individual need, but take shape in the form of proactive—and political—advocacy for changes in the built and human environment.

One particularly important kind of "stretch" that can be given to the representative dimensions of ministry is the idea of a minister being not only representative of the local church *in* the wider community in which it is set and of which it is part, but also of the minister as—on occasion—representative *of* that wider community.[3] Stephen Cherry's searing narrative of the ordeal of accompanying the family, the trial, and the neighborhood after a young boy's body turned up, dismembered, in the town's canal is one important testimony to the possibility of such ministry.[4] As the English Anglican Cherry recounts, in his experience not only did the church building become a major public focus for shock and grief and rage and sorrow in the unfolding of horrible circumstances, but so also did he as parish priest, receiving spoken and unspoken permission to speak and act on the local community's behalf. Such costly and demanding ministry is surely an exemplary instance of being, in Lathrop's terms, a gathering place for communal encounter with wider meaning. Yet Cherry's experience is embedded in the opportunities of Establishment—albeit, even as Sarah Coakley insists, the legacy of Establishment is an ecumenical opportunity in the UK,[5] and as Alan Billings argues, in any case only survives in any tradition as "Establishment-lite."[6] Of course, this Establishment context is not part of experience elsewhere—including both Australia and the USA, the settings in which this book took shape—and cultural exegesis of other contexts is inevitably in numerous respects different from that of Britain. Those contexts also merit careful ongoing analysis, not least so that the potential of pastoral carers to offer service in the (of course disparate, fluxing) "public" is not underestimated. Underambitious notions of the scope of ministerial representation can be corrected by contextual attention to possibilities for "mythical moreness."

---

3. For a strong argument, see Alan Billings, *Making God Possible: The Task of Ordained Ministry Present and Future* (London: SPCK, 2010), 49.

4. Stephen Cherry, "Representation," in *Praying for England: Priestly Presence in Contemporary Society*, ed. Samuel Wells and Sarah Coakley (London: Continuum, 2008), 21–41.

5. Coakley, "Prayer, Place and the Poor."

6. Billings, *Making God Possible*, 155: "As long as a critical mass of the British people are able to associate themselves with Christianity, establishment can still make sense and can still be justified. The choice is not 'the secular state' or 'establishment'; there is a very British, middle way: establishment lite."

Perhaps what public ministers are able to offer is something like "visible vulnerability"? Known in their local communities, they one way or another make themselves visible, and so heighten their own vulnerability to the varied, sometimes inchoate, demands that persons may place before Christian symbols embodied by (or swirling around) pastors. We see something of this in narratives like Stephen Cherry's, in moments of community strife when the request comes for clergy presence at protest marches in city parks, and in persons' tentative steps to participate in "Ashes to Go" at subways stations, when the church's ritual riches for the opening of Lent are carried into the streets. As visibly vulnerable, public ministers invite engagement with whatever confusion about Christian faith may be present in wider society, as well as with the possibly half-articulate aspirations—within as well as beyond congregational life—of what Christian commitment involves. Public ministers place themselves into ambiguous spaces with the simple daring expectation that they will in some way be able to be "useful." We might recall Austin Farrer's ordination sermon, "Walking Sacraments":

> No one's calling shows them up as a priest's does. And indeed . . . there is nothing to prevent a priest being a very ordinary man; most priests must always have been so. Being a priest does not make a man more helpful to his fellow-Christians in matters of wisdom or of kindness; what it does do is give his fellow Christians a right to his services. It might well be that the woman next door to you had greater gifts for teaching small children than the school-mistress: but that doesn't mean that you can expect her to teach your little ones for you. You've a right to the school-mistress's services; she's given herself over to be eaten alive by the children of the place. And so with the priest: go on, eat him alive, it's what he's for; you needn't feel shy of devouring his time, so long, of course, as it's to fulfil a need.[7]

---

7. Compare Austin Farrer, "Walking Sacraments," in *The Truth-Seeking Heart: Austin Farrer and His Writings*, ed. Ann Loades and Robert MacSwain (Norwich: Canterbury Press, 2006), 140–41.

Perhaps something related to this is artfully elaborated in Graham Hughes's vision of "limping priests,"[8] with his allusion to priests who are limping of course drawing on Genesis 32's narrative of Jacob wrestling with the divine. Hence, Hughes avers that "the public sign of one who wrestles with God is *dislocation*." He is concerned to uphold the "primary dignity, worth and validity of the ministry of Christ's baptized people," which he deems to require "delimitation," and he suggests that this might happen through steps including that "those very particular ministerial tasks for which some ministers need to show particular aptitudes and which require an especial authorization (ordination) need to be both articulated and adhered to with scrupulous exactitude" and that "large, nonspecific terms . . . (such as 'leadership') or the generic use of 'ministry' (when 'ordained ministry' is intended) should be abandoned." He also insists "a necessary part of the delimitation or focus inherent in a renewed understanding of ordination for our times will have to do with the preparation (formation) of people for such ministry."[9]

With what Hughes says here, I strongly concur, and his last point just cited leads to reflection on *formation* and the institutional setting in which this book emerged: seminaries. "Seminary," then, is a place that, as this book draws to a close, I want to place next to hospital, altar, and road work. Seminaries are a place where many ordained and lay ministers learn at least some of their ministerial practice, or at least how they might think about it. Yet seminaries are not what they more often were—residential, largely populated by males, many of whom were relatively recently out of college. Latterly, seminary education might, at least for some, involve significant portions of learning done online or in intensive residentials during which students may not even stay together or spend much time together. The effectiveness for ministerial formation of these newer forms of seminary participation is not yet known, but then it needs to be acknowledged that uncertainty about

8. Graham Hughes, "Limping Priests: Ministry and Ordination," *Uniting Church Studies* 8 (2002): 1–13. See also Stephen Burns, "'Limping Priests' Ten Years Later: Formation for Ordained Ministry," *Uniting Church Studies* 17 (2011): 1–16, on which I draw in what follows.
9. Hughes, "Limping Priests," 6.

this sits alongside a perhaps growing dissatisfaction with older forms of residential learning which are sometimes perceived to too much remove students from contexts of active ministry.

One constant (thus far) of seminary experience in recent years has been the necessity of somehow undertaking fieldwork as part of the course of learning. For many students, this includes opportunity to undertake CPE. For as long as this arrangement holds, seminary experience will involve at least the elsewhere of some fieldwork parish or other setting of ministry. As such, fieldwork constitutes a crucial part of seminary education beyond the physical or virtual classroom. But there are many other dimensions of seminary curricula to consider.

### Curricula Issues

Even in more settled, residential settings, curriculum for ministry places great demands on seminaries, and any attempt to fulfill the demands will require attention much wider than whatever can be learned in classrooms, from lectures and books. It is not only that in seminaries one way or another worship takes place alongside study of worship, in various respects persons live in or by one means or another make some attempt to form community in ways which are not necessarily incumbent on students in secular universities. Further, practical theology is likely to have a larger role in seminaries than many university-based theology programs. More, though: chapel, fieldwork in which "practical skills" for ministry can be tested, and questions of vocation toward an ecclesial (and hopefully wider) context all shape the environment. What some commentators on curriculum call the "climate and culture" in which classes and reading take place need scrutiny, so that what is being taught can be imbibed from how the community gathers and is ordered, the models of leadership that are in place, the ethos and practices of the community assembling for worship, arrangement and use of common spaces, listening and review processes for students and leaders, how and when hospitality is extended—and by whom, and much else. In newer online contexts of learning, need for scrutiny of such things does not disappear, but may in fact become more acute. For all that a principal vocation of a seminary might involve dealing with books and teaching classes, formation takes places in a community practicing ministry.

With something of this wider view, the Association of Theological Schools, the major North American body for accrediting seminaries, talks of an "entire" or "total curriculum," a "theological curriculum, comprehensively understood."[10] And because language of formation for ministry can sometimes be used quite opaquely, it is helpful to distinguish different dimensions, as is commonly done in identifying three aspects: theological education, spiritual formation, and practical training. The three are themselves criss-crossing and sloping, but untangling them (at least for long enough to think about them separately) helps to highlight where there may be a lopsided emphasis on one, or an absence or deficit of another. Classrooms and books are most obviously categorized in the former dimension of formation, "theological education," and this by no means covers the full stretch of curriculum seminaries need to try to set in place. At the same time, it needs to be acknowledged that fieldwork (perhaps in hospitals) can contribute greatly to spiritual formation—as can books, and I hope that reflection in this present book might be its own witness to that.

Other mappings of curriculum are also helpful. Elizabeth Conde-Frazier's "thoughts on curriculum" are particularly valuable for thickening understanding. She considers Charles Foster's notions of "pedagogies of performance" (teaching and learning of practices through observation, imitation, and rehearsal) and "pedagogies of formation" (how spiritual and professional identity is formed within and outside the classroom,

---

10. See http://www.ats.edu/uploads/accrediting/documents/general-institutional -standards.pdf 3.2, 3.2, 3.2.1, 3.2.2.3. For further reflection on the work of seminaries, see Stephen Burns, "Formation for Ordained Ministry: Out of Touch?" in *Aboriginal Australia and the Unfinished Business of Theology: Crosscultural Engagement*, ed. Jione Havea (New York: Palgrave, 2014), 151–66, and Stephen Burns, "When Seminaries Get Stuck," in *Liturgy in Postcolonial Perspectives: Only One Is Holy*, ed. Claudio Carvalhaes (New York: Palgrave, 2015), 255–66.

in worship, service, spiritual disciplines, and so on).[11] She also discusses Kathleen Calahan's notions of "vertical" curriculum (how students move from introductory to more advanced studies), "horizontal" curriculum (the impact different parts of students' experience have on one another), alongside her own sense of a "diagonal" curriculum (concerned with integration of learning with life experience, identity, privilege, and discrimination, such as we have explored in chapter 5).[12]

Highly valuable, too, is Maria Harris's distinction between what she terms "a curriculum of education" and "a curriculum of schooling." The former refers to the interplay of several modes of learning, including "education in, to, and by service, community, proclamation, worship, and teaching." By contrast, schooling is a term she reserves to "only one of the many valuable forms through which education occurs, that form which generally happens in a place called a school, a form focused on processes of instruction, reading of texts, conceptual knowledge, and study."[13] Seminaries, not least in their concern for spiritual formation and practical training, are engaged in curricula of education, albeit as classrooms and books also plant them firmly in curricula of schooling. What is more, Harris also distinguishes three powerful modes of curriculum—its explicit, implicit, and null aspects. The explicit curriculum "refers to what is actually presented, consciously and with intention. It is what we say we are offering, what is found in our table of contents." The implicit curriculum, in contrast, "refers to the patterns or organization or procedures that frame the explicit curriculum: things like attitudes or time spent or even the design of a room." In the implicit curriculum, classrooms and books are seen in a wider context, in terms of the institutions, communities, and bodies (even buildings) in which they work, which might otherwise be "left implicit, not spoken of or paid attention as part of the educational

11. Elizabeth Conde-Frazier, "Thoughts on Curriculum as Formational Praxis for Faculty, Students and Their Communities," in *Teaching for a Culturally Diverse and Racially Just World*, ed. Eleazar S. Fernandez (Eugene, OR: Cascade, 2014), 134–35.
12. Conde-Frazier, "Thoughts," 133–34.
13. Maria Harris, *Fashion Me a People: Curriculum for the Church* (Louisville, KY: Westminster John Knox Press, 1989), 64–65. The following paragraphs quote from pages 64–69 of Harris's book.

process." The implicit curriculum invites questions about the congruence of what communities with an explicit curriculum practice in light of what they teach, what they say about themselves, how they promote and advertise themselves, and much else. Harris defines the null curriculum thus: "a paradox. This is the curriculum that exists because it does not exist; it is what is left out, but the point of including it is that ignorance or the absence of something is not neutral. It skews the balance of options we might consider, alternatives from which we might choose, or perspectives that help us to see." So while the implicit curriculum is what does not have attention drawn to it until it is named as also relevant, the null curriculum is "areas left out," "procedures left unused." Examples Harris calls attention to include "two-way dialogue, extensive consultation . . . and participation in decisions by all concerned."

Harris's categories lead to very interesting questions as in seminaries, congruence between different curricula becomes a test of their integrity.[14] Elizabeth Conde-Frazier herself develops Harris's categories in ways that add texture, asserting that "social location, gender, race, and ethnicity . . . all . . . very much form the curriculum."[15] Some of this we have explored in part two of this book. But Conde-Frazier also points to "gestures, intonations, inflections, vocal volume, manner of pacing and the many different looks I give my students," all things that are also crucial matters in liturgy. "How I dress" is also, according to Conde-Frazier, part of the curriculum, along with "the relationship between teacher and student," and not just architecture but classroom arrangement are formative, as well as processes to which students are subject, "the distance that professors take from the subject they teach," the "policies operating that socialize us," "the make-up of the board . . . and the values inherent in their decisions." Dress and space are matters that we have touched, while questions of policies, boards, and organization invite analogs in

---

14. For more on congruence in seminary curricula, see Stephen Burns, "School or Seminary? Theological Education and Personal Devotion," *St. Mark's Review* 210 (2009): 79–95.

15. Conde-Frazier, "Thoughts," 128. The following paragraphs quote from pages 128–29 of Conde-Frazier's essay.

the realms we have been exploring. All of this as it intersects needs great care, not least because as Conde-Frazier claims: "The nature of the relationships that we have with one another as staff, professors and administrators is felt by our students and it teaches them an entire content about power and powerlessness, class, gender, and race relations." What Conde-Frazier says of teachers also applies to pastors: Their social location, their clothes, the looks they give, the nature of their relating, and so on, are indeed part of their "curriculum," what others are able to learn from and with them. They too must be congruent in terms of what they say and how they behave: As the *New Zealand Prayer Book* brilliantly bluntly puts it to ordinands, "You must be what you proclaim." At least some of their capacity, or not, to find such congruence may depend on what they experience in seminary and how it has—or has not—fostered what Karl Rahner called the "ever closer intimacy between [the ordinands] and [their] office."[16]

Pastoral theologians as well as their students in seminary need to be concerned with such matters. For what Daniel Aleshire suggests is true of pastoral ministers is as true of the seminaries in which pastors are formed:

> People tend to assess the work of ministers and priests in terms of three broad questions: Do they truly love God? Do they relate with care and integrity to human beings? Do they have the knowledge and skills that the job requires? . . . Not only do people ask them, they tend to ask them in this order. If the answer to the first question is "no," people don't even proceed to the second and third questions.[17]

### Limping Priests

Graham Hughes's view of what formation requires, above, is largely concerned with questions of *focus*. Seminaries, whether residential, virtual, or in some kind of hybrid mode, must teach this. Hughes suggests that

---

16. Karl Rahner, quoted by Andrew D. Mayes, "Priestly Formation," in *Developing Faithful Ministers: A Theological and Practical Handbook*, ed. Tim Ling and Lesley Bentley (London: SCM Press, 2012), 30.

17. Daniel Aleshire, *Earthen Vessels: Hopeful Reflections on the Work and Future of Theological Schools* (Grand Rapids, MI: Eerdmans, 2008), 31.

formation must "prepare . . . the candidate to live out, or live within, the limitations which this particular [i.e., ordained] ministry demands."[18] He understands that to concentrate on "the enabling, or inculcation, of a requisite humility precisely in knowing one's necessary power" as what he calls storyteller, mystagogue, and carer. "Inculcation" is a key word, and relates to the climate and culture of the seminary itself. Making his own connections with some of the terrain covered in this book, Hughes relates ministry of the word not only to storytelling but the kind of listening that is at the heart of the therapeutic tradition: "Storytellers . . . must be able to read foreign languages, they must be as diligent students of human nature as they are of ancient texts, and they must have a pastor's heart." Obviously, as a liturgical theologian, concerned that formation should focus on worship, Hughes relates presidency to the ancient idea of mysta- gogy: "Sacramental leader[ship] . . . means a great deal more than being able to say the words and perform the actions at the table or the font." Rather, he says, it is "only derivatively (though importantly) to do with presiding at the table of communion," and "vastly transcends 'administer- ing the sacraments.'" His more expansive understanding involves

> the mystagogue [as] . . . someone able to lead her or his people relatively safely through the "tremendous mystery" which is the condition of our life and through the local mystery which is each Lord's Day worship. No one can successfully or responsibly undertake the latter who is not deeply acquainted with, yet not overwhelmed by, the former.

Hughes, in these ways, closely relates both attending to words and celebrating sacramentality with pastoral care:

> No one can break open the Word into people's lives (or con- versely, open lives to the light of God's Word), nor can one safely lead the same people through the terror and ecstasy which await us at life's boundaries, if one does not know these people—deeply, intimately, "carefully."

---

18. Hughes, "Limping Priests," 6. The following paragraphs quote from pages 6–14 of Hughes's article.

Hughes's vision of the task of formation for ordained ministry is the sharpest I know of. What kind of formation does it require? How can institutions and experiences be structured to facilitate and foster it?

Hughes is surely right that ministers need

> to know deeply within themselves . . . how to occupy positions of power, but loosely; not be . . . afraid actually to preside in worship and then be . . . able to let it go; [and] to be free for dangerous, incisive—threatening even—interpretations of the community's disposition and yet in a way that is empowering, grace-full; to know that some human agent must speak the word of absolution or blessing in God's stead or on Christ's behalf; and yet, in all this, knowing one's own all-too-immediate frailty.[19]

Yet while affirming Hughes's vision of the broken symbol of ordained ministry as that of "limping priests" (as he says, "the only effective priest is a priest who limps"[20]), I would nevertheless also invite attention to the question of "reach"[21] alongside his question of focus, and I hope that *Pastoral Theology for Public Ministry* might encourage such reflection. Formation that strategically employs the like of Clinical Pastoral Education to nurture candidates' confidence of their potential to find a role beyond the sanctuary, and that, for example, nurtures candidates' capacity to make explicit links between public and contextual theology and the sociopolitical contexts of care are, in my view, helpful and necessary complements to the like of learning sensitivity to representative ministry through deft embrace of liturgical turnings and other robust liturgical gestures. This is not so much an argument with Hughes, but a stretching of his perspectives, amplifying his own articulate sense of the ways in which pastoral carers[22] are always themselves but not only themselves, and may yet be able to be a vivid sign in other public spaces as well as at the altar.

---

19. Hughes, "Limping Priests," 13.
20. Hughes, "Limping Priests," 14.
21. Stephen Pickard uses the phrase "the question of reach" in his *Theological Foundations for Collaborative Ministry* (Aldershot: Ashgate, 2008), 85–108.
22. Hughes's argument in "Limping Priests" is of course especially concerned with ordained pastoral carers.

# RECOMMENDED READING

*Notes throughout the text above draw in a wider literature than is listed below. This list, however, brings together reading from pastoral and practical theology, liturgical theology, ministerial formation, and Anglican identity.*

Aleshire, Daniel O. *Earthen Vessels: Hopeful Reflections on the Work and Future of Theological Schools*. Grand Rapids, MI: Eerdmans, 2008.

Bartlett, Alan. *A Passionate Balance: The Anglican Tradition*. Maryknoll, NY: Orbis, 2007.

Billings, Alan. *Making God Possible: The Task of Ordained Ministry Present and Future*. London: SPCK, 2010.

Bradshaw, Paul. *Rites of Ordination: Their History and Theology*. Collegeville, MN: Liturgical Press, 2014.

———. *Two Ways of Praying: Introducing Liturgical Spirituality*. London: SPCK, 1995.

Brown, Rosalind, and Christopher Cocksworth. *On Being a Priest Today*. Cambridge, MA: Cowley, 2002.

Burns, Stephen. *Liturgy*. SCM Studyguide. London: SCM Press, 2006.

———. *Worship and Ministry: Shaped Towards God*. Melbourne: Mosaic Press, 2012.

Burns, Stephen, ed. *Journey*. Norwich: Canterbury Press, 2008.

Burns, Stephen, and Clive Pearson, eds. *Home and Away: Contextual Theology and Local Practice*. Eugene, OR: Pickwick Press, 2013.

Cartledge, Mark. *Practical Theology: Charismatic and Empirical Perspectives*. Carlisle: Paternoster, 2003.

Chapman, Justine Allain. *Resilient Pastors: The Role of Adversity in Healing and Growth*. London: SPCK, 2012.

Chase, Steven. *The Tree of Life: Models of Christian Prayer*. Grand Rapids, MI: Baker Academic Press, 2005.

Cooper-White, Pamela, and Michael Cooper-White. *Exploring Practices of Ministry*. Minneapolis, MN: Fortress Press, 2014.

Countryman, C. William. *The Poetic Imagination: An Anglican Tradition*. Maryknoll, NY: Orbis, 2007.

Croft, Steven. *Ministry in Three Dimensions: Ordination and Leadership in the Local Church*. London: DLT, 2008.

Doehring, Carrie. *The Practice of Pastoral Care: A Postmodern Approach*. Louisville, KY: Westminster John Knox Press, 2006.

Dowling, Ronald L., and David R. Holeton, eds. *Equipping the Saints: Ordination in Anglicanism Today*. Dublin: Columba Press, 2006.

Dykstra, Robert C., ed. *Images of Pastoral Care: Classic Readings*. St. Louis, MO: Chalice Press, 2004.

Earey, Mark. *Beyond Common Worship: Anglican Identity and Liturgical Diversity*. London: SCM Press, 2013.

———. *Worship That Cares: An Introduction to Pastoral Liturgy*. London: SCM Press, 2012.

Esterline, David V., and Ogbu Kalu, eds. *Shaping Beloved Community: Multicultural Theological Education*. Louisville, KY: Westminster John Knox Press, 2006.

Forrester, Duncan B. *Theological Fragments: Essays in Unsystematic Theology*. London: Continuum, 2005.

———. *Truthful Action: Explorations in Practical Theology*. Edinburgh: T & T Clark, 2000.

Foster, Charles R., et al. *Educating Clergy: Teaching Practices and Pastoral Imagination*. San Francisco, CA: Jossey-Bass, 2005.

Frame, Tom, ed. *Called to Minister: Vocational Discernment in the Contemporary Church*. Canberra: Barton Books, 2009.

Graham, Elaine L. *Transforming Practice: Pastoral Theology in an Age of Uncertainty*. London: Mowbray, 1996.

———. *Words Made Flesh: Essays in Pastoral and Practical Theology*. London: SCM Press, 2009.

Holeton, David R., ed. *Growing in Newness of Life: Christian Initiation in Anglicanism Today*. Toronto: Anglican Book Centre, 1993.

———. *Our Thanks and Praise: The Eucharist in Anglicanism Today*. Toronto: Anglican Book Centre, 1998.

Jagessar, Michael N., and Stephen Burns. *Christian Worship: Postcolonial Perspectives*. Sheffield: Equinox, 2011.

Kaye, Bruce. *An Introduction to World Anglicanism*. Cambridge: Cambridge University Press, 2007.

Kujawa-Holbrook, Sheryl, and Karen Montagno, eds. *Injustice and the Care of Souls: Taking Oppression Seriously in Pastoral Care*. Minneapolis, MN: Fortress Press, 2009.

Kwok Pui-lan et al., eds. *Anglican Women on Church and Mission*. New York: Morehouse, 2012.

Lartey, Emmanuel Y. *In Living Color: An Intercultural Approach to Pastoral Care and Counseling*. London: Mowbray, 1997.

———. *Pastoral Theology in an Intercultural World*. Cleveland, OH: Pilgrim Press, 2006.

Lathrop, Gordon W. *The Pastor: A Spirituality*. Minneapolis, MN: Fortress Press, 2006.

Ling, Tim, and Lesley Bentley, eds. *Developing Faithful Ministers: A Theological and Practical Handbook*. London: SCM Press, 2012.

Mayes, Andrew D. *Spirituality in Ministerial Formation: The Dynamics of Prayer in Learning*. Cardiff: University of Wales Press, 2009.

Meyers, Ruth A. *Missional Worship, Worshipful Mission: Gathering as God's People, Going Out in God's Name*. Grand Rapids, MI: Eerdmans, 2014.

Miller-McLemore, Bonnie. *Christian Theology in Practice: Discovering a Discipline*. Grand Rapids, MI: Eerdmans, 2012.

Miller-McLemore, Bonnie, ed. *The Wiley-Blackwell Companion to Practical Theology*. Chichester: Wiley-Blackwell, 2013.

Monro, Anita, and Stephen Burns, eds. *Public Theology and the Challenge of Feminism*. London: Routledge, 2014.

Moore, Zoe Bennett. *Introducing Feminist Perspectives on Pastoral Theology* Sheffield: Sheffield Academic Press, 2002.

Pattison, Stephen. *The Challenge of Practical Theology: Selected Essays*. London: Jessica Kingsley, 2007.

———. *A Critique of Pastoral Care*. London: SCM Press, 2000.

———. *Pastoral Care and Liberation Theology*. Cambridge: Cambridge University Press, 1994.

Pratt, Andrew. *Practical Skills for Ministry*. SCM Studyguide. London: SCM Press, 2010.

Pritchard, John. *The Life and Work of a Priest*. London: SPCK, 2007.

Ramsey, Nancy, ed. *Pastoral Care and Counseling: Redefining the Paradigms*. Nashville, TN: Abingdon Press, 2004.

Reddie, Anthony G. *Is God Colourblind? Insights from Black Theology for Christian Ministry*. London: SPCK, 2010.

Sharp, Melinda McGarrah. *Misunderstanding Stories: Toward a Postcolonial Pastoral Theology*. Eugene, OR: Pickwick Press, 2013.

Slee, Nicola, and Stephen Burns, eds. *Presiding Like a Woman*. London: SPCK, 2010.

Stevenson-Moessner, Jeanne, and Teresa Snorton, eds. *Women Out of Order: Risking Change and Creating Care in a Multicultural World*. Minneapolis, MN: Fortress Press, 2009.

Stoddart, Eric. *Advancing Practical Theology: Critical Discipleship in Disturbing Times*. London: SCM Press, 2014.

Thompsett, Fredrica Harris, ed. *Looking Forward, Looking Backward: Forty Years of Women's Ordination*. New York: Morehouse, 2014.

Weil, Louis. *Liturgical Sense: The Logic of Rite*. New York: Seabury Press, 2012.

White, Susan J. *The Spirit of Worship: The Liturgical Tradition*. Maryknoll, NY: Orbis, 2000.

Wilkey, Glaucia Vasconcelos, ed. *Worship and Culture: Foreign Country or Homeland?* Grand Rapids, MI: Eerdmans, 2014.

Willimon, William, ed. *Pastor: A Reader*. Nashville, TN: Abingdon Press, 2002.

Wimberly, Edward P. *African American Pastoral Care: The Politics of Oppression and Empowerment*. Cleveland, OH: Pilgrim Press, 2006.

Woodward, James, and Stephen Pattison, eds. *The Blackwell Companion to Pastoral and Practical Theology*. Oxford: Blackwell, 2000.

# ACKNOWLEDGMENTS

I am grateful for permission to reprint various copyright materials, as follows:

The National Assembly Office of the Uniting Church in Australia for permission to use extracts of *Uniting in Worship 2* (Sydney: Uniting Church Press, 2005). Used by kind permission.

The General Synod of the Anglican Church in Aotearoa New Zealand and Polynesia for extracts of *A New Zealand Prayer Book—He Karakia Mihinare o Aotearoa* (Auckland: Collins, 1989). Used by kind permission.

Gwydion Thomas and Kunjana Thomas for R. S. Thomas, "The Priest," © Eloide Thomas, 2002. Used by kind permission.

Nicola Slee and SPCK for Nicola Slee, "Conversations with Muse," from Nicola Slee, *Praying Like a Woman* (London: SPCK, 2004). Used by kind permission. I am grateful to Nicola, an inspiring teacher, colleague and friend, for so much else.

Nancy Bryan at Church Publishing has been helpful and deft in her comments on a draft of this book, and Ryan Masteller and Milton Brasher-Cunningham are both to be thanked for their work on seeing the book through the production process.

Judith and Dominic are much to be thanked, with much love, as always.

I dedicate this book to the marvelous seminarians of St. James's, Cambridge, and the Crossing, Boston Cathedral.

# ABOUT THE AUTHOR

Stephen Burns is Stewart Distinguished Lecturer in Liturgical and Practical Theology at Trinity College Theological School, Melbourne, Australia, where he also serves as Co-ordinator of Ministerial Formation and Associate Dean. He has taught in the USA (at Episcopal Divinity School, Cambridge) and the UK (at the Queen's Foundation for Ecumenical Theological Education, Birmingham). He studied at the Universities of Durham and Cambridge and is a priest in the orders of the Church of England. His publications include *Postcolonial Practice of Ministry* (coeditor with Kwok Pui-lan, 2016), *Liturgical Spirituality* (editor; Seabury Press, 2013), *Worship and Ministry* (2012), *Christian Worship: Postcolonial Perspectives* (coauthor with Michael N. Jagessar, 2011), *Worship in Context* (2006), and *Liturgy* (SCM Studyguide; 2006).

.

www.ingramcontent.com/pod-product-compliance
Lightning Source LLC
Jackson TN
JSHW080852211224
75817JS00002B/13